Contents

Unit 1: Ideas

- [ ] **Week 1:** Choosing a Strong Idea 3
  Convention: Periods
- [ ] **Week 2:** Writing a Topic Sentence 8
  Convention: Sentence Capitalization
- [ ] **Week 3:** Using the "5 Ws" to Add Details 13
  Convention: Contractions
- [ ] **Week 4:** Choosing Strong Details 18
  Convention: Question Marks
- [ ] **Week 5:** Sticking to Your Topic 23
  Convention: Commas in Place Names

Unit 2: Organization

- [ ] **Week 1:** Beginning, Middle, and End 28
  Convention: Exclamations
- [ ] **Week 2:** Putting Things in the Right Order 33
  Convention: Commas After Introductory Words and Phrases
- [ ] **Week 3:** Grouping Together Ideas and Details 38
  Convention: Using *Their*, *There*, and *They're*
- [ ] **Week 4:** Grouping by How Things Are Alike or Different 43
  Convention: Underline Book Titles
- [ ] **Week 5:** Choosing Which Way to Organize Your Writing 48
  Convention: Comparatives and Superlatives

Unit 3: Word Choice

- [ ] **Week 1:** Choosing Strong Verbs and Adverbs 53
  Convention: Using *To*, *Too*, and *Two*
- [ ] **Week 2:** Choosing Colorful Adjectives 58
  Convention: Commas Between Adjectives
- [ ] **Week 3:** Telling Exactly Who or What 63
  Convention: Singular Possessive Nouns

© Evan-Moor Corp. • EMC 6793 • Daily 6-Trait Writing

☐ Week 4: Using Similes and Metaphors 68
   Convention: Possessive Pronouns

☐ Week 5: Getting the Reader's Attention 73
   Convention: Commas in Dates

Unit 4: Sentence Fluency

☐ Week 1: Varying Your Sentences 78
   Convention: Using *Saw* and *Seen*

☐ Week 2: Combining Sentences 83
   Convention: Commas in Compound Sentences

☐ Week 3: Revising Run-on and Rambling Sentences 88
   Convention: Comma Usage

☐ Week 4: More Ways to Combine Sentences 93
   Convention: Commas in Complex Sentences

☐ Week 5: Writing a Smooth Paragraph 98
   Convention: Irregular Past Tense Verbs

Unit 5: Voice

☐ Week 1: Examining Different Writing Voices 103
   Convention: Contractions

☐ Week 2: Using Formal and Informal Language 108
   Convention: Quotation Marks in Dialogue

☐ Week 3: Creating a Mood 113
   Convention: Capitalization in Poetry

☐ Week 4: Writing from Different Points of View 118
   Convention: Prefixes *un-* and *dis-*

☐ Week 5: Developing Your Own Voice 123
   Convention: Commas in Dialogue

Proofreading Marks 128

Week 1 • Day 1

 **Ideas** Choose a strong idea. Make your idea specific.

A. Read each student's story ideas. Underline the one that is stronger and more specific.

1. John's story ideas:
   a. My sister's teddy bear
   b. Finding my sister's lost teddy bear

2. Brianna's story ideas:
   a. Why I like Grandmother's house in Mexico City
   b. Visiting Mexico

B. Read the three ideas below. Choose one to make more specific. Circle it and write the specific idea.

   Ideas: bike riding

   movies

   baking cookies

   A more specific idea: _____

   _____

C. Read the sentences. Circle the periods.

   Rocky wrote about seeing a bridge in Oakland. The bridge is called the Bay Bridge. It is 43,500 feet long.

Week 1 • Day 2

 **Ideas** Choose a strong idea. Make your idea clear.

A. Julia is making a scrapbook with photos of a camping trip. Help her write a clear idea about each photo. Write the idea in a complete sentence. The first one is done as an example.

Idea: Riding

Clearer Idea: <u>Here I am riding a horse for the first time.</u>

Idea: Camping

Clearer Idea: _____

Idea: Swimming

Clearer Idea: _____

Idea: Eating

Clearer Idea: _____

B. Proofread each sentence you wrote.

Week 1 • Day 3

 **Ideas** Choose a strong idea. Tell about something that is important to you.

A. Hunter races BMX bikes with his family. Which ideas do you think Hunter would probably want to write about the most? Write an *X* by them.

 _____ 1. How to play baseball

 _____ 2. Bike-racing gear

 _____ 3. What my dad and I do on race day

 _____ 4. Training your dog

 _____ 5. The first BMX race I won

B. Think about what you like to do on the weekends. Choose one thing and write it on the line. Then think of three specific ideas you could write about it. Write your ideas in complete sentences with periods.

I like to _____

Specific Ideas:

1. _____
   _____

2. _____
   _____

3. _____
   _____

Week 1 • Day 4

 **Ideas** — Choose a strong idea. Narrow it down.

Think about fun things you like to do with friends. Complete the triangle. Narrow down your ideas into one specific idea.

Start with a general idea.

fun with friends

Narrow it down.

Make it more specific.

6   IDEAS   Daily 6-Trait Writing • EMC 6793 • © Evan-Moor Corp.

Week 1 • Day 5

 Write about something specific that you like to do with friends. Be sure that each statement ends with a period.

Week 2 • Day 1

 **Ideas** — Each paragraph should have a topic sentence. It tells the reader what the paragraph is mainly about.

A. Read this book report. Circle its topic sentence. Use proofreading marks to fix the sentences that do not begin with a capital letter.

Stellaluna

Stellaluna is a story about a little baby bat. one day, Stellaluna falls out of her tree and into a bird nest. She becomes part of the birds' family. But she still wants to do the things that bats do. she even hangs upside down like a bat! The mother bird tells Stellaluna she can't act like a bat. She has to act like a bird. in the end, Stellaluna decides that it's OK to be a bat and still be friends with the birds.

B. This book report is missing its topic sentence. Read the report. Then write a topic sentence for it.

Where the Wild Things Are

At dinnertime, Max acts like a monster. His mother sends him to his room. then he gets angry and imagines that he is in a boat. he sails to another world that has wild monsters! When Max finally comes home, he thinks he has been gone for a year and is sad. But he hasn't been gone that long! it's still dinnertime, and Max is happy again.

Topic Sentence: _____

_____

C. Reread the book report in Activity B. Use proofreading marks to fix the sentences that do not begin with a capital letter.

Week 2 • Day 2

 **Ideas** — Each paragraph should have a topic sentence.

A. Read this friendly letter. Circle the paragraph that is missing a topic sentence. Use proofreading marks to fix the sentences that do not begin with a capital letter.

> September 12, 2008
>
> Dear Zachary,
>
> Last weekend, my Aunt Sara took us to the Jackson City Library. She picked us up on Saturday morning. when we got there, we ran up the steps. There was a giant fountain with a statue. the statue was of a bear reading a book. People sat by the fountain and read. Some people were eating lunch. Pigeons also stood by the fountain. they were waiting to steal people's food!
>
> You can take books off the shelves. you can sit in a beanbag chair. You can listen during the story hour. You can put on headphones and listen to books on CDs.
>
> I would like to see you soon. Do you ever go to the library? Maybe some day I will see you there.
>
> Your friend,
> Josie

B. Reread the paragraph you circled. Write a topic sentence for it.

_____

_____

_____

Week 2 • Day 3

 **Ideas** Each paragraph should have a topic sentence. You can use a web to plan your topic sentence and supporting sentences.

Read the sentences in the box. Use the sentences to complete the web.

Sentences

One book is called John Henry.
Today I read two new books.
One book is called 365 Penguins.
I got the books from my brother's shelf.
I read one book in class and the other after school.

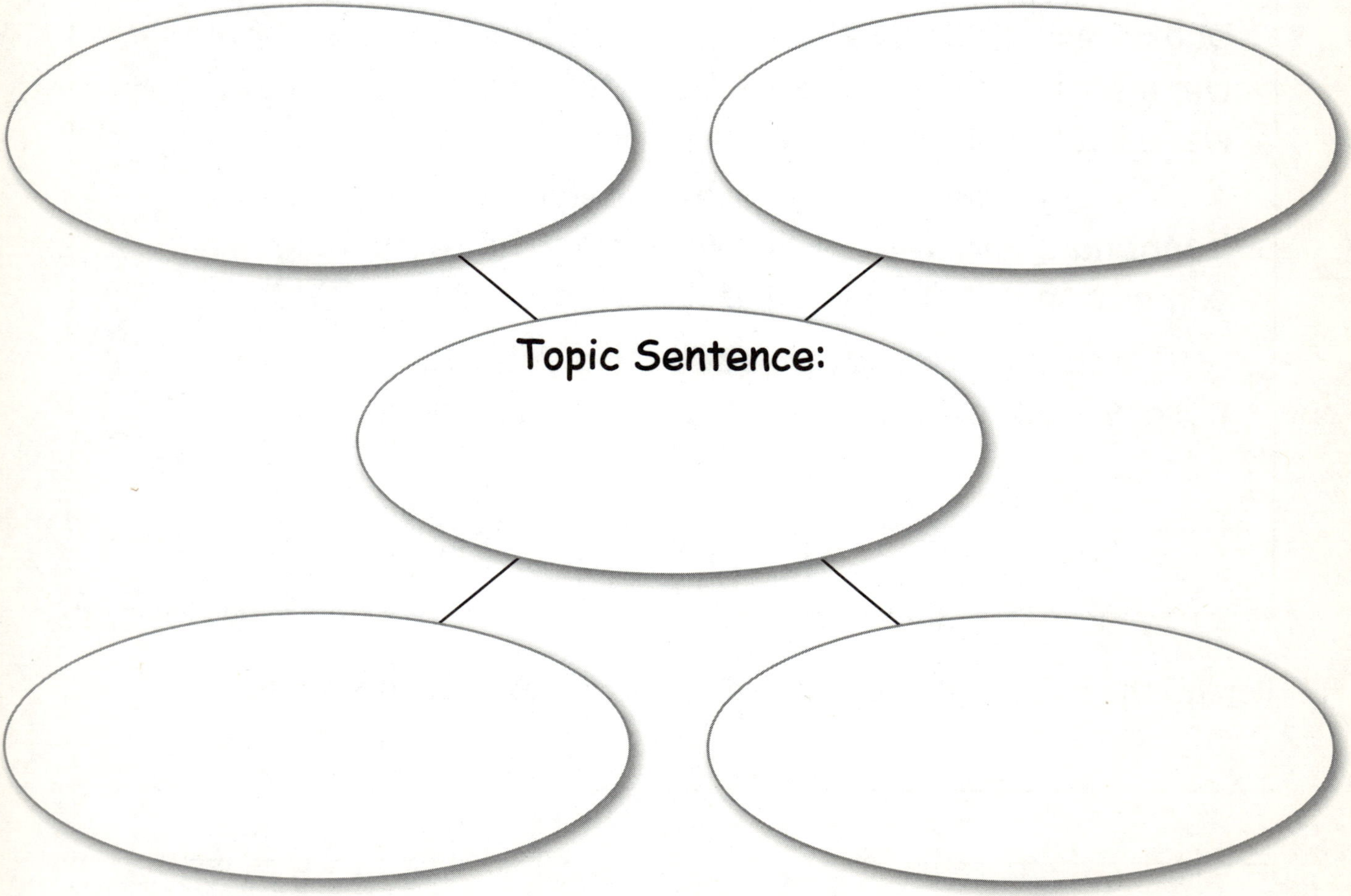

Topic Sentence:

Week 2 • Day 4

 **Ideas** You can use a web to plan sentences for a paragraph.

Think of a place where you like to read. In the center circle, write a topic sentence about the place. In the outer circles, write supporting sentences that give details about the place. Be sure to start each sentence with a capital letter.

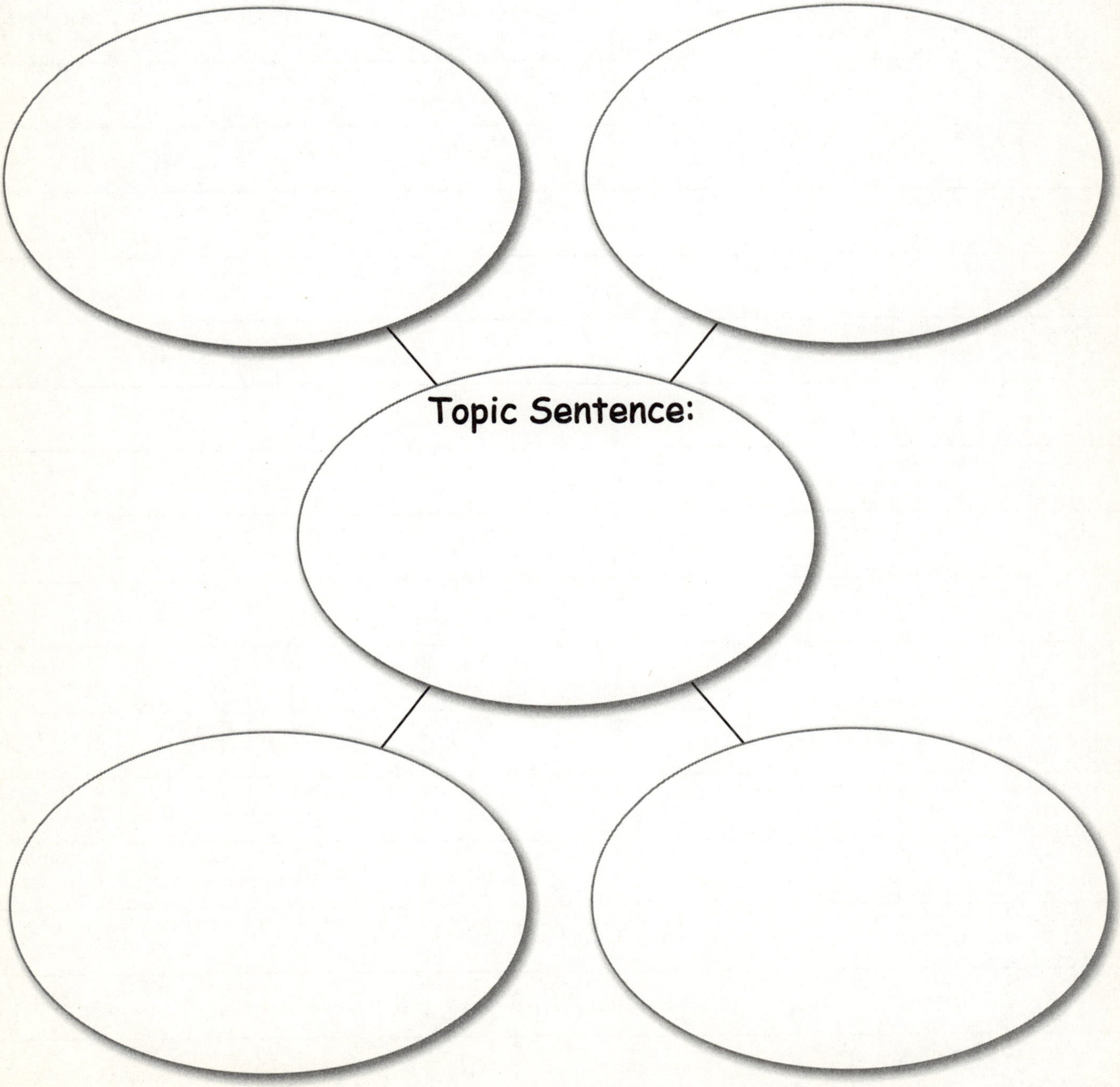

Topic Sentence:

Week 2 • Day 5

 **Ideas** Write a paragraph that describes your favorite place to go to read. Be sure to begin each sentence with a capital letter.

Week 3 • Day 1

 **Ideas** Details make your writing more interesting. Add details telling *who* and *what*.

A. Read these articles from a school newspaper. One article gives interesting details telling *who* and *what*. Draw a star next to it.

News from Room 7

We had Dictionary Day this week. Everyone got a new dictionary! We learned about a man who wrote a dictionary. We found some of our names in the dictionary.

News from Room 12

All the third-grade classes got new dictionaries on October 16. That is Dictionary Day. It is also the birthday of Noah Webster. He wrote the first American dictionary. It was fun to look for our names in the dictionary. We found *Victor, Grace, Lily,* and *Mason*.

B. Look at these details from the second article. What kind of details are they? Write *who* or *what* next to each one.

1. All the third-grade classes   _____

2. Noah Webster   _____

3. The first American dictionary   _____

4. Victor, Grace, Lily, and Mason   _____

Week 3 • Day 2

 **Ideas** — A good writer includes details that tell *when*, *where*, and *why*.

A. Read the paragraph. Circle the details that tell *when*. Underline the details that tell *where*. Draw two lines under the details that tell *why*.

School was very different one hundred years ago. In farming states such as Iowa, many families lived in the country. The children went to school in one-room schoolhouses. They came from far and wide, because there weren't many schools. Children didn't take a bus to school. They walked, sometimes for miles. One teacher taught all the grades, because the students were all different ages. The teacher went to school at dawn. She had to light the wood stove. She used chalk to write the lessons on a blackboard. At eight o'clock, she rang a bell to start school. She rang it again at the end of the day.

B. Write a sentence about your school. Use a detail that tells *when*, *where*, or *why*.

_____

_____

_____

C. Write the two contractions in the paragraph above that are made from the word *not*.

_____   _____

14 IDEAS   Daily 6-Trait Writing • EMC 6793 • © Evan-Moor Corp.

Week 3 • Day 3

 **Ideas** Use the "5 Ws" to make your writing interesting. Tell *who, what, when, where,* and *why.*

A. Write the missing details to tell *who, what, when, where,* or *why.*

Details		
to Danville Junior High	fifty years ago	cellphone
my grandma Beth	it was against the rules	at 4:00
her friend Selma	in Selma's locker	skirt

When _____ (who) _____ went to school, some things were different. It was _____ (when) _____. Grandma went _____ (where) _____. She wore a _____ (what) _____ or dress every day. That's because _____ (why) _____ for girls to wear pants. Also, she did not have a _____ (what) _____. It was not invented yet. So if she wanted to send _____ (who) _____ a message, she had to put a note _____ (where) _____. They often walked home together after school _____ (when) _____. Grandma says it's hard to believe how much has changed.

B. Read each pair of words. Write their contractions. Then circle those contractions in the paragraph.

that + is = _____   it + is = _____

Week 3 • Day 4

 **Ideas** Use the "5 Ws"—*who, what, when, where,* and *why*— to help you plan your writing.

Think back to your first day of school this year. What details can you remember about it? Fill in the chart.

The First Day of School

Who was there:	
What you did:	
When it took place:	
Where things happened:	
Why you liked or didn't like it:	

Week 3 • Day 5

 **Ideas** Use your chart to write about the first day of school this year. Use a contraction made from *not* or *is*, such as *didn't* or *that's*. Be sure to use an apostrophe.

Week 4 • Day 1

 **Ideas** — Choose strong details to interest your reader.

A. Read the paragraph about Emma's pet. Underline the details.

Do you know what a guinea pig is? A guinea pig isn't really a pig. It is a rodent, just like hamsters and rats. What is a guinea pig like? My guinea pig Isabelle is a small, gentle pet. She lets me hold her and brush her fur.

B. Read what Anna wrote about her pet. She needs to add more details. Look at the picture and list three details she could add.

Do you like dogs? I do. My dog Spot is three years old. We got him when he was a puppy. He is a fun pet to have.

Details:

1. _____
2. _____
3. _____

C. Circle the question marks in the paragraphs above.

Week 4 • Day 2

 **Ideas** Use sensory details to describe how something looks, sounds, or feels.

A. Read this riddle about a fairy tale pet. Underline the sensory details about the pet. Then answer the riddle.

My pet is soft and white. She is magical. I just say the magic word, and my pet squawks. Then she lays a golden egg for me! Where did this wonderful animal come from? I climbed a tall beanstalk and took her from the giant's castle.

Who am I? _____

Who is my pet? _____

B. Think of a character from the story "Little Red Riding Hood." Write a riddle that gives clues about the character. Describe how the character looks and sounds. Give sensory details about what he or she does.

This character has _____

This character _____

Who is this character? _____

C. Change this sentence to a question. Remember to use a question mark at the end.

You are a wolf!

_____

IDEAS 19

Week 4 • Day 3

 **Ideas** — Choose strong details to support your topic. Give examples to explain your ideas.

A. Read Ava's paragraph about why birds make good pets. Then complete the chart with the examples Ava gave for each idea.

>   Has a dog ever said "hello" to you? A bird can! Birds are smart animals. They are easy to train. Some birds, such as parakeets and parrots, can even learn to talk. Birds are also easy to take care of. They don't need to go on walks. You don't have to brush or wash them. Birds do not take up a lot of space or cost a lot of money to take care of. They live in cages, and their food is very cheap. I think birds make the best pets.

Ideas	Examples
Birds are smart animals.	
Birds are easy to take care of.	
Birds do not take up a lot of space or cost a lot of money to take care of.	

B. Would you want to have a pet snake? Write why or why not. Give a strong detail that supports your idea.

_____

_____

_____

Week 4 • Day 4

 **Ideas** Choose strong details to help you plan your writing.

If you could have any pet, what would it be? Write details in the web about your ideal pet. It could be a pet you already have or one you'd like to get.

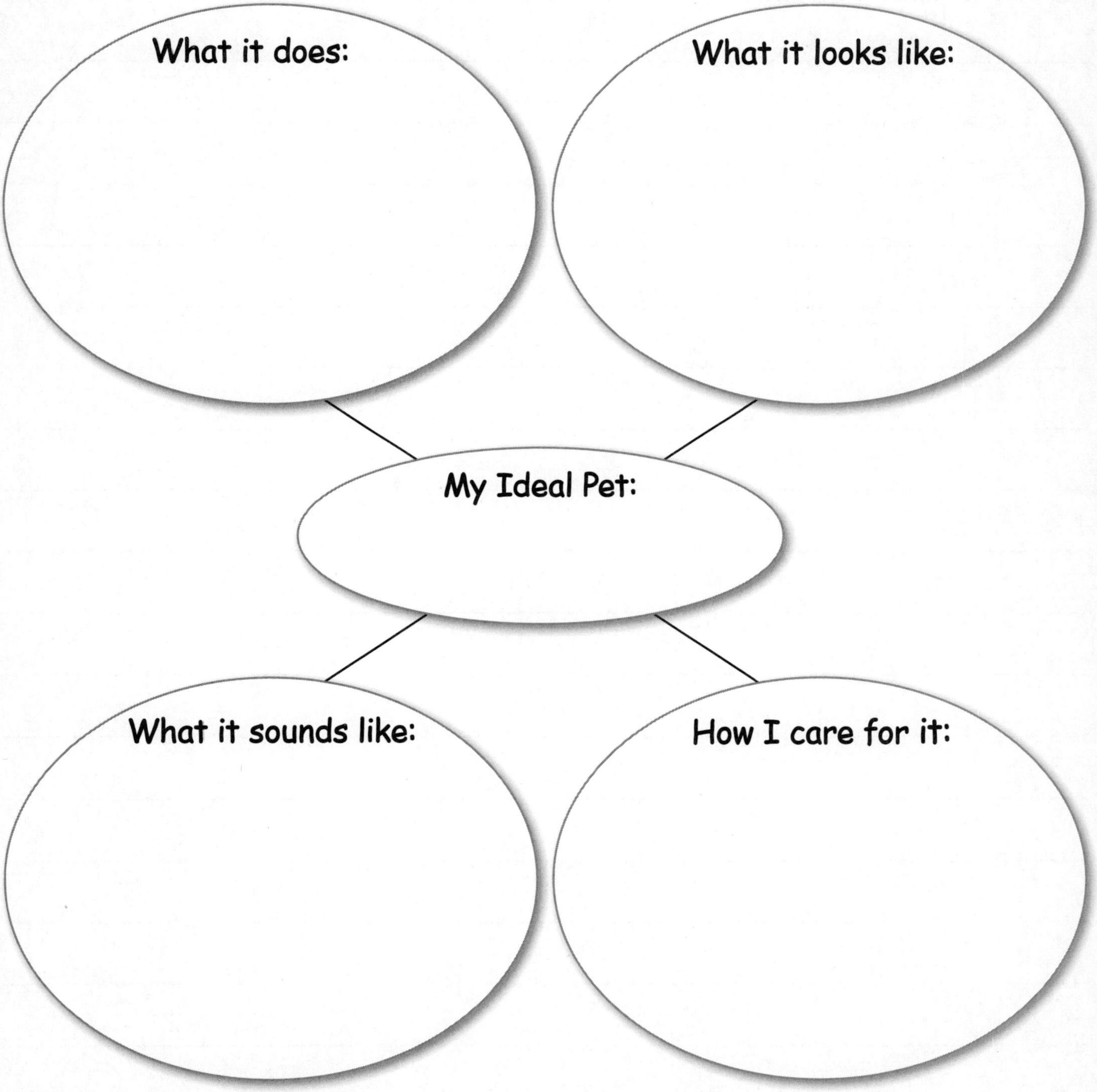

- What it does:
- What it looks like:
- My Ideal Pet:
- What it sounds like:
- How I care for it:

Week 4 • Day 5

Ideas — Write a paragraph that describes your ideal pet, but don't give away what kind of animal it is! At the end of your paragraph, write "What is it?" Be sure to use a question mark at the end of the question.

Week 5 • Day 1

 **Ideas** Include only details that stick to your topic.

A. Read the sentences under each picture. Cross out the sentence that does not stick to the topic of the picture.

We packed the car in the morning.
We wanted to leave early.
We had pizza for dinner yesterday.

We went to the Gateway Arch in St. Louis, Missouri.
Last year we visited Austin, Texas.
It looked like a giant metal ribbon.

After a while, I got hungry.
We stopped to get some lunch.
I live in Chicago, Illinois.

Camping in the mountains is fun.
We saw the Mississippi River.
The river is very wide!

B. Write the missing commas in these place names.

1. Las Vegas Nevada
2. Buffalo New York

Week 5 • Day 2

 **Ideas** Take out details that don't stick to your topic.

A. Read Glenn's letter to his pen pal, Serena. Cross out the sentences that do not tell about where Glenn lives.

> Dear Serena,
>
> I live in Burlington, Vermont. It is the largest city in Vermont. Burlington is near a lake and mountains. My birthday is in the summer. The lake is named Lake Champlain. It's fun to sail on the ocean. On the other side of the lake is New York. Do you like hockey? We also have the Green Mountains. Can you guess why they are called the Green Mountains? They are covered with trees! I like books about mummies.
>
> Your friend,
> Glenn

B. Write two sentences about where you live. Include the name of your city and state. Remember to place a comma between the city and state.

_____

_____

_____

Week 5 • Day 3

 **Ideas** Take out details that do not stick to your topic.

A. Anthony is planning a paragraph about his birthday party. Read his web. Cross out the details that do not stick to his topic.

- had cake and ice cream
- New Year's Day is soon.
- party at Grandma's in Brooklyn, New York
- blew out candles
- went to the Grand Canyon on vacation
- **My Birthday Party**
- had a piñata
- had strep throat last year
- The Science Museum has a big volcano.
- opened presents
- cousins Ben and Marley came

B. Match each city to its state. Write the paired cities and states on the lines. Remember to use commas to separate the city and state.

City	State
Dallas	Florida
Miami	Ohio
Cleveland	Texas

1. _____
2. _____
3. _____

Week 5 • Day 4

 **Ideas** Write only details that stick to your topic.

A. Think about a birthday party you have had or have been to. Use the web to list details about the decorations, food, and activities.

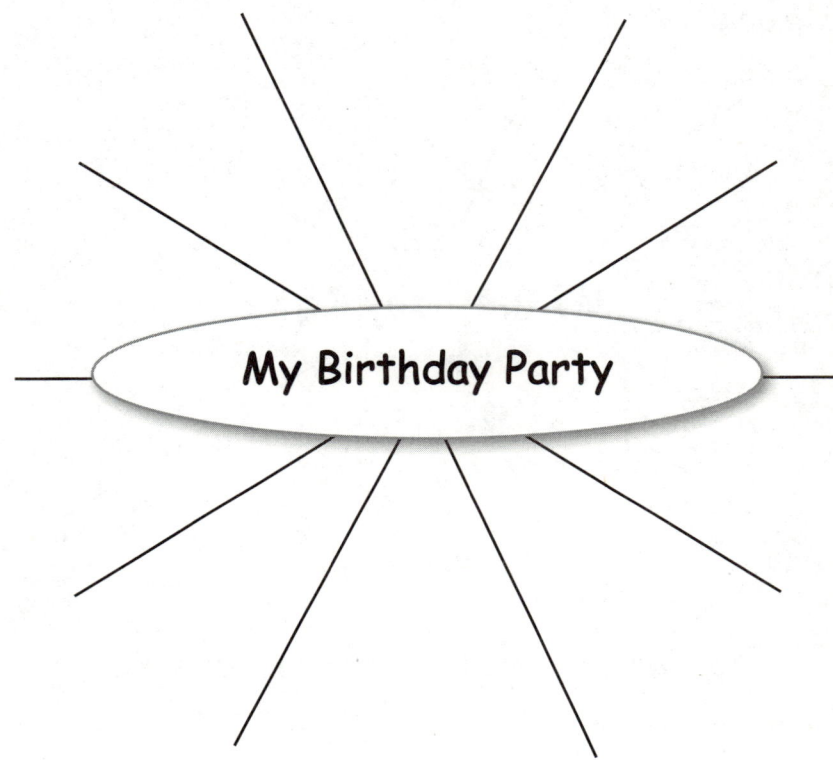

B. Trade webs with a partner. Check each other's webs to make sure that each detail sticks to the topic. Cross out any details that don't stick to the topic.

Week 5 • Day 5

 **Ideas** Write a description of a birthday party. Make sure your details stick to your topic. Include the city and state where the party took place. Be sure to use a comma to separate the place names.

_____
_____
_____
_____
_____
_____
_____
_____
_____
_____
_____
_____
_____
_____
_____
_____
_____
_____

City and State: _____

Week 1 • Day 1

 **Organization** Write a bold beginning to grab your reader's attention.

A. Read each pair of story beginnings. Underline the beginning that grabs your interest and makes you want to read on. Then write the method the writer used to begin the story. Choose from this list:

- Use a quotation.
- Use sound words.
- Create a feeling of mystery.
- Ask a question.

1. a. Joe was walking his dog in the moonlight.
   b. Something was different about the sky that night as Joe walked his dog.
   Method: _____

2. a. Bong! Bong! Bong! The huge Tower Bell rang out across the land.
   b. The bell in the tower was ringing.
   Method: _____

3. a. Yesterday, nothing went right.
   b. Have you ever had one of those days when nothing goes right?
   Method: _____

4. a. "I'm amazing!" my brother exclaimed, after doing ten cartwheels.
   b. My brother did ten cartwheels yesterday!
   Method: _____

B. Find the exclamations in Activity A. Circle each exclamation point.

Week 1 • Day 2

 **Organization** — Write a middle that is interesting and makes sense between the beginning and ending.

Read the beginning and ending of this story. Draw and write what happens in the middle. Make it exciting! Use at least one exclamation.

Mean Mauler and Me

The bell rang at 3 o'clock. Everyone but Ben cheered. He had to walk home past Mr. Warren's place.

Mr. Warren had a dog named Mauler. Some kids said Mauler was part wolf. Every time Ben walked by Mr. Warren's house, Mauler chased him down the street.

Ben slowly trudged home. When he got near Mr. Warren's house, he darted behind a lamppost. Then he dashed under a bush. Suddenly, Ben heard a deep growl.

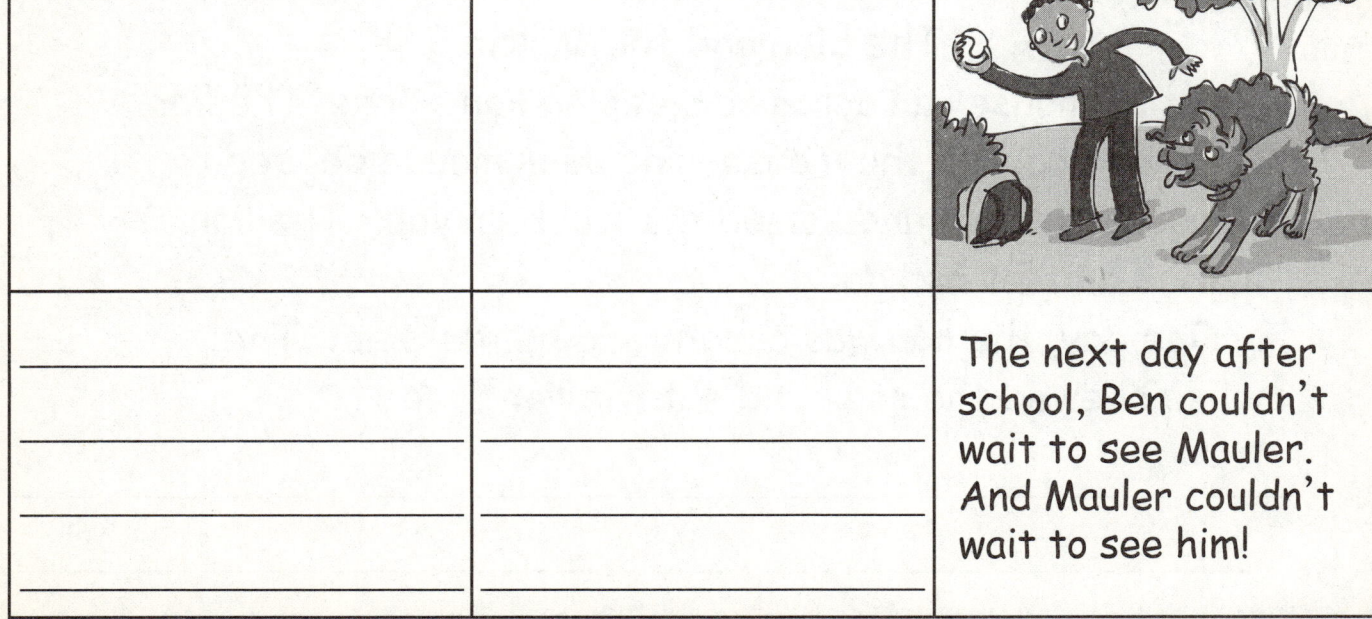

The next day after school, Ben couldn't wait to see Mauler. And Mauler couldn't wait to see him!

Week 1 • Day 3

 **Organization** Write an ending that wraps up the events in your story.

A. Read the fable. Then choose an ending from the box and circle it.

The Goose and the Golden Egg

Once there was a man who had a very special goose. Every day, it laid a golden egg. The man sold the eggs. This made him rich! But he thought he wasn't getting rich fast enough. So he decided he would get all the golden eggs at one time by cutting open the goose. He found no eggs.

Possible Endings

(**wise thought**) The goose was dead. And the man who wanted it all had nothing.

(**quotation**) "I've killed the goose for nothing!" cried the man. "I will never be greedy again!"

(**conclusion**) The man had killed the goose for nothing. He would never try to get rich quickly again.

B. Write an ending to this fable about kindness.

The Lion and the Mouse

A tiny mouse ran across a sleeping lion's nose. The lion awoke and caught the mouse. The poor mouse begged, "Please let me go, and someday I will help you." The lion laughed and let him go.

One day, the lion was caught in a hunter's net. The mouse chewed the rope and set the lion free.

_____

_____

Week 1 • Day 4

 Write a complete story with a beginning, middle, and ending.

Think of a fairy tale that you know. Plan to tell your own version of it. Write or draw what happens in the beginning, middle, and end.

Beginning

↓

Middle

↓

Ending

Week 1 • Day 5

 Rewrite a fairy tale with a clear beginning, middle, and end. Use an exclamation in your story. Be sure to end it with an exclamation point.

Week 2 • Day 1

 **Organization** When you write, be sure to put everything in the right order.

A. The instructions below are out of order. Look at the pictures. Then:
- Number the steps to put them in the right order.
- Write the order word *First, Next, Then, Now,* or *Finally* at the beginning of each step.

How to Make a Wind Vane

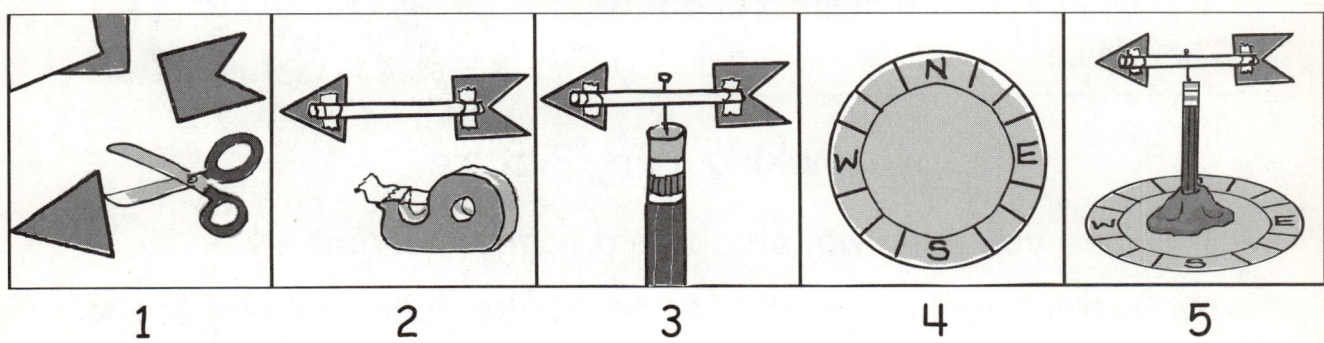

1   2   3   4   5

Number	Step
____	_____, tape the arrow pieces to a straw's ends.
____	_____, stand the pencil in clay on the plate. Take your wind vane outside to spin in the wind!
____	_____, cut out an arrow's point and tail.
____	_____, push a pin through the middle of the straw and stick the pin into a pencil eraser.
____	_____, write *N, S, E,* and *W* on a paper plate to show North, South, East, and West.

B. Circle the commas after the introductory order words in Activity A.

Week 2 • Day 2

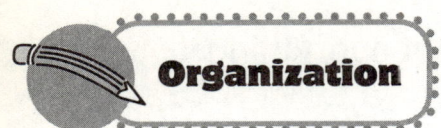 **Organization** — When you write about how to do something, be sure to put the steps in the right order.

A. Read the instructions for making a fog picture. Complete the sentences with the phrases in the box. Use the order words as clues to where each phrase belongs.

Phrases
- Now, cover
- Finally, fold
- Then, glue
- Next, cut out
- To begin, cut out

Making a Fog Picture

Have you ever woken up on a foggy morning when everything looked gray? You can make your own fog scene! You will need gray, brown, and black paper. You will also need glue, scissors, and waxed paper. _____ _____ some brown hills and glue them onto a sheet of gray paper. _____ two black trees and glue them in front of the hills. _____ the picture with a sheet of waxed paper. Glue it along the edges. _____ some more hills and trees on top of the waxed paper. _____ paper strips over the edges to make a frame for your picture.

B. Read the sentences. Write the missing commas.

First Daniel gave the glue to Maria. Then Maria passed the glue to Thomas. Finally Thomas handed it to Hannah.

Week 2 • Day 3

 **Organization** — When you describe something that happened, be sure to put the events in the correct order.

A. Jamar's class made a chart of the weather last week. Study the chart. Use it to write a description of how the weather changed throughout the week. Write at least three sentences. Be sure to place commas after introductory words and phrases.

Our Weather Chart

 Monday	 Tuesday	 Wednesday	 Thursday	 Friday
partly cloudy	rainy	snowy	sunny	sunny

_____
_____
_____
_____
_____
_____
_____

B. Look back at the sentences you wrote in Activity A. Check to make sure that you wrote commas after the introductory words and phrases. Circle the commas, and add them if necessary.

ORGANIZATION 35

Week 2 • Day 4

 **Organization** — When you describe something that happened, be sure to put the events in the correct order.

Imagine that you had a mixed-up weather day. It went from spring to summer to fall to winter, all in one day! What was your day like? How did the weather change your plans? Write your ideas on the chart.

A Mixed-up Weather Day

Time	Weather	Activity
Morning		
Lunchtime		
Afternoon		
After School		
Evening		

Week 2 • Day 5

 **Organization**

Write about a day when the weather was all mixed up! Be sure to write commas after introductory words and phrases.

Week 3 • Day 1

 **Organization** — Group together similar ideas and details to make your writing easy to understand.

A. Read what Lani wrote about the languages spoken in Hawaii. Notice how she grouped certain ideas and details together. Draw one line under the details about the English language. Draw two lines under the details about the Hawaiian language.

Let's Talk

My state, Hawai`i, is different from other states. There are two official languages! They're English and Hawaiian. English is the language spoken in schools. It is also used in business and the government. Hawaiian was spoken here before Hawai`i became a state. It was the language of the native people and their rulers. It started to fade away, but now it is being taught again. Let me teach you some Hawaiian words. **Lei** (lay) means "a necklace of flowers." **Mahalo** (mah-HA-lo) means "thank you." **Aloha** (ah-LO-ha) is a greeting. It means "love."

B. Write the word from the story that completes each of these sentences.

1. _____ are two official languages!

2. _____ English and Hawaiian.

3. It was the language of the native people and _____ rulers.

Week 3 • Day 2

 **Organization** Group together details so your reader can follow your ideas.

Read the story and the details in the box. Correct the misspelled word in the box. Then write each detail where it belongs in the story.

Details

We also planted squash seeds.

There keeping weeds and bugs away.

Those plants were called the "three sisters."

A "Three Sisters" Garden

Native people sometimes planted corn, beans, and squash together. _____

_____ We planted a "three sisters" garden at school. We made mounds of dirt and planted corn seeds in each one. After two weeks, we planted beans around the corn.

_____

Guess what is happening! The bean plants are climbing up the corn. They're putting plant food in the soil to help the corn grow. The squash is growing big, prickly leaves.

_____

The three sisters are helping each other grow!

Week 3 • Day 3

 **Organization** Group together details so your reader can follow your ideas.

A. Help Tyler organize his details for a report about the Comanche people. Write the idea that each detail tells about—*clothing* or *homes*.

The Comanche

Clothing   Homes

1. Men and women wore clothes made of deerskin. _____

2. They're homes, called tepees, were made of buffalo hide. _____

3. A tepee was like a tent. This made it easy to move. _____

4. The tepees provided good protection from the weather. _____

5. They wore leather moccasins on there feet. _____

B. Correct the two misspelled words in Tyler's details above.

C. Organize Tyler's details about Comanche homes to finish this paragraph.

The Comanche people used animal skins to make their homes.

_____

_____

_____

Week 3 • Day 4

 **Organization** — Group together similar ideas and details.

Native peoples had different languages. They made their own clothes and homes. They planted and hunted for food. Plan a paragraph about how your family lives today. Use the web to organize your details.

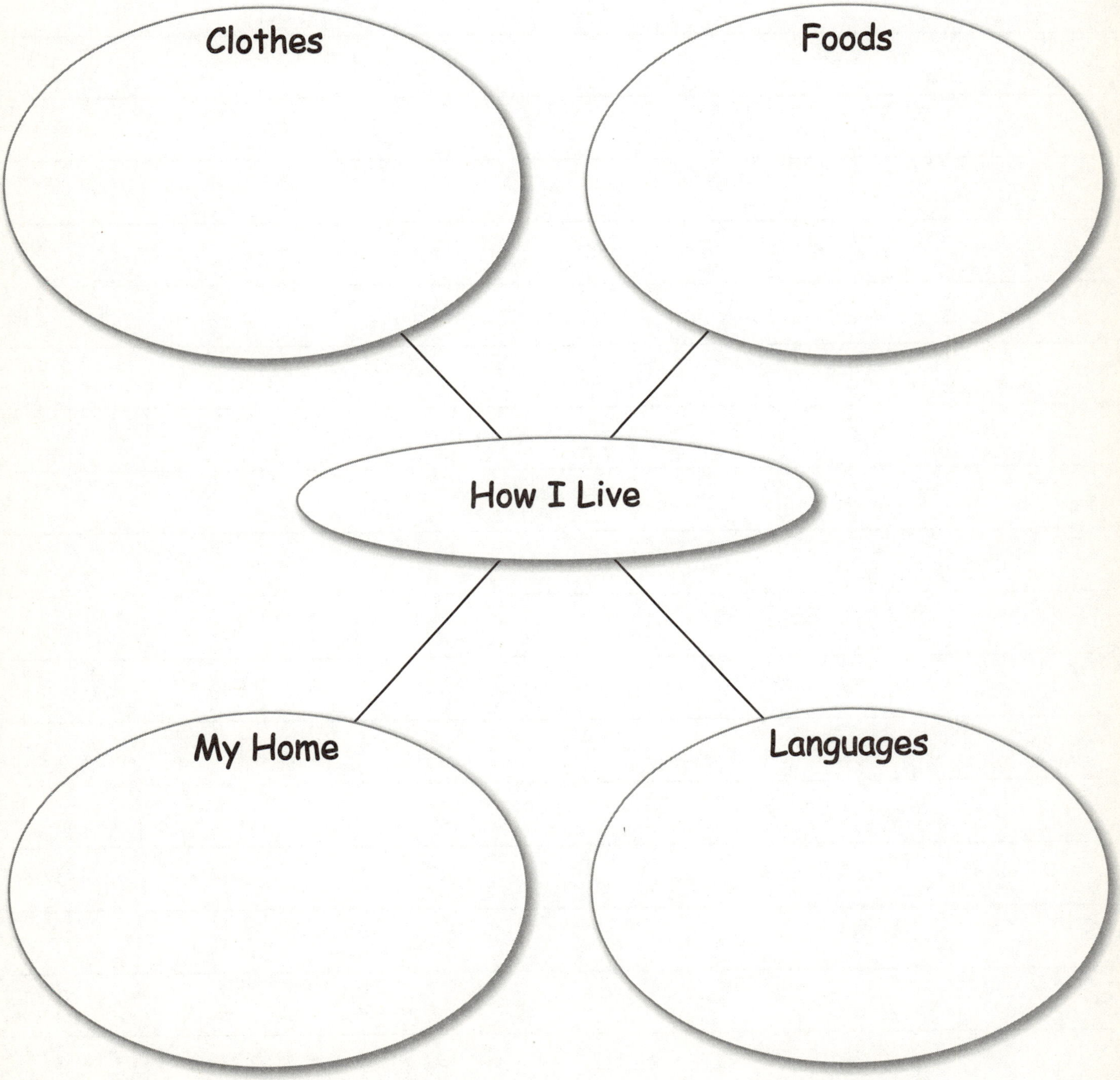

- Clothes
- Foods
- How I Live
- My Home
- Languages

ORGANIZATION

Week 3 • Day 5

 **Organization**

Write a paragraph about how you live. Use your web from Day 4 to help you organize your details.

Be sure to use *their, there,* and *they're* correctly.

Week 4 • Day 1

 **Organization** When you compare two or more things, organize your writing by how they are alike or different.

A. Read this paragraph about Faith Ringgold and Jerry Pinkney. Draw a line under the sentences that tell how they are alike.

Both Faith Ringgold and Jerry Pinkney wanted to be artists when they were children. And, in fact, they both illustrated books about Harriet Tubman. Ringgold's book is entitled Aunt Harriet's Underground Railroad in the Sky. Pinkney's book is entitled Minty: A Story of Young Harriet Tubman.

B. Read the paragraph. Fill in the chart to show how the two artists are different.

Ringgold paints stories on fabric quilts for her books. She has created 14 children's books so far. Unlike Ringgold, Pinkney is famous for his watercolor paintings. He has painted pictures for more than 100 children's books!

	Ringgold	Pinkney
Type of Art		
Number of Books		

C. Underline the book titles in this sentence.

The books Tar Beach by Faith Ringgold and The Talking Eggs by Jerry Pinkney have each won many awards.

Week 4 • Day 2

 **Organization** — When you compare two or more things, organize your writing by how they are alike or different.

A. Sofia is writing a comparison of her two favorite books. Read the ideas she wrote in the Venn diagram.

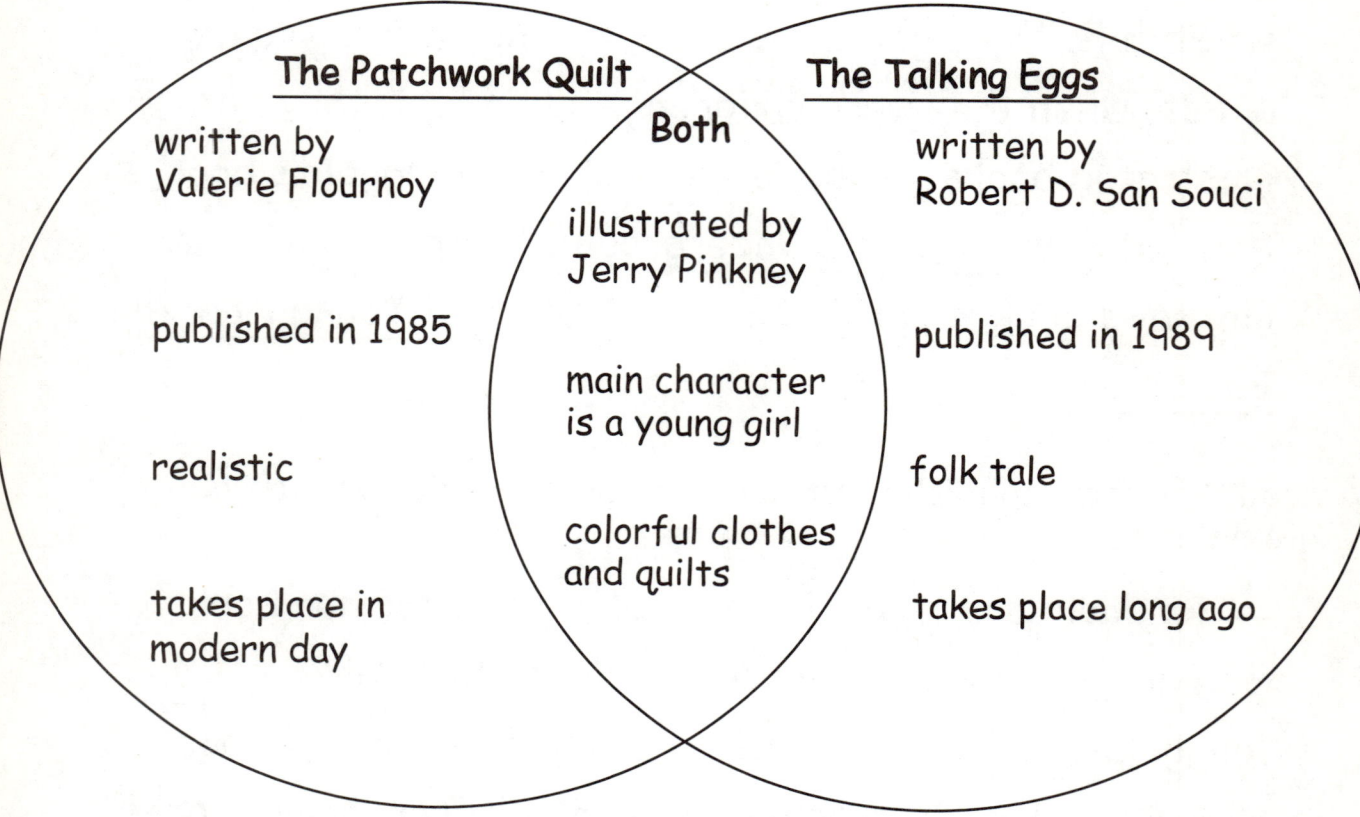

B. Write a sentence telling one way the books are alike.

_____

_____

C. Write a sentence telling one way the books are different. Be sure to underline the titles of the books.

_____

_____

Week 4 • Day 3

Organization — Use signal words to help your reader follow your organization.

A. Logan is writing about how two buildings are alike and different. Fill in the signal words from the box to complete Logan's paragraph.

Library in Turkey   Museum in Spain

Signal Words		
but	like	however
both	unlike	

These pictures show a library and a museum. The library and the museum are _____ famous buildings. However, they are very different from each other. The library is ancient, _____ the modern museum. Also, the library has many straight lines, _____ the museum has wiggly lines. The library was built entirely of stone. _____, the museum was made of metal, glass, and stone. _____ the museum, the library has rectangle-shaped windows.

B. Complete the paragraph about how a library and a bookstore are alike and different. Use the signal words to help you.

A library and a bookstore are similar. For example, _____.

Also, _____.

However, _____.

Week 4 • Day 4

 **Organization** — Organize your writing by how things are alike or different.

Plan a report about two books you like. Think about the main characters. How are they alike? How are they different? Write your ideas in the diagram.

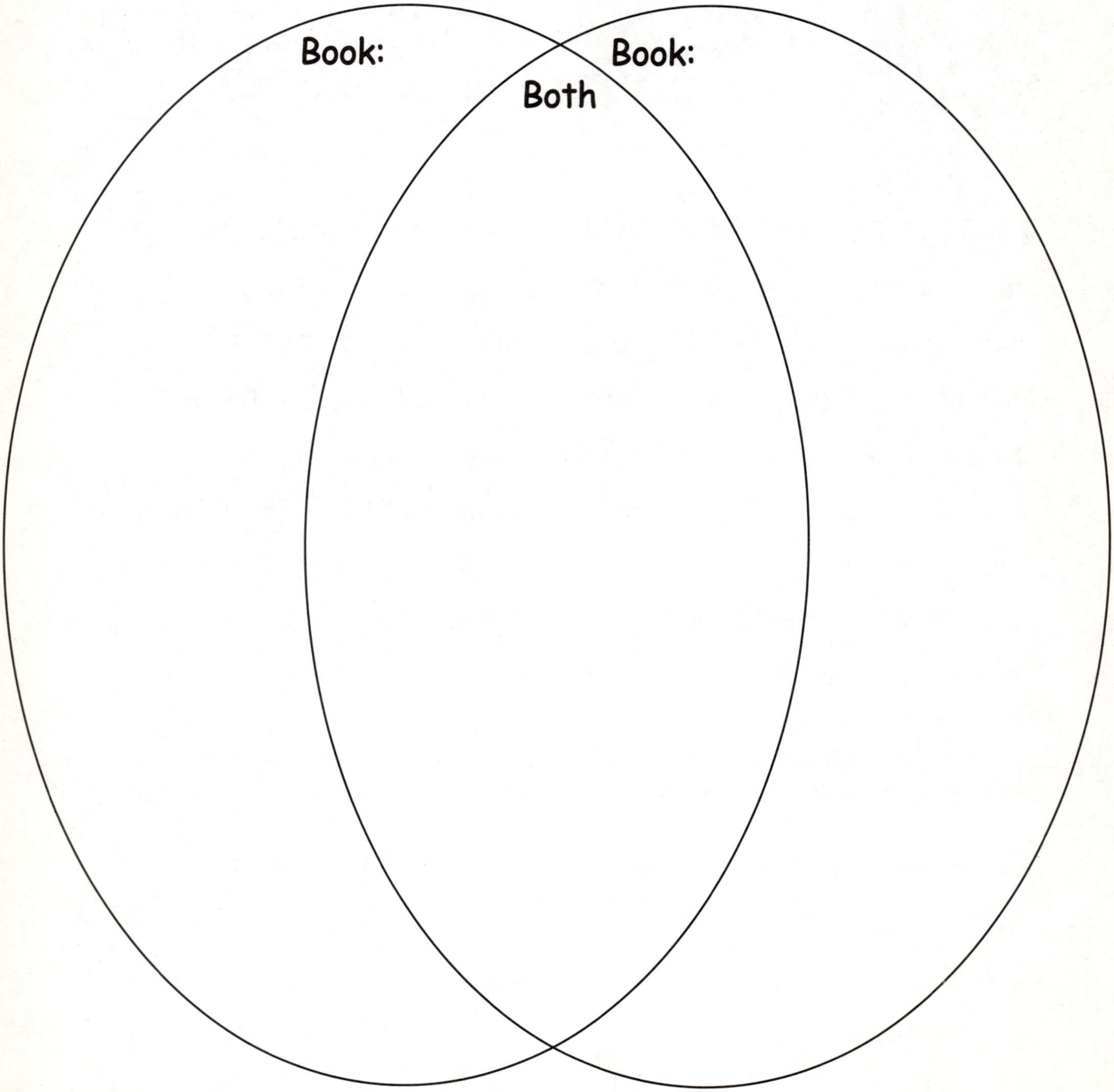

Book: _____   Both   Book: _____

Week 4 • Day 5

 Write a report comparing and contrasting the main characters in two of your favorite books.

Be sure to underline the titles of the books.

Week 5 • Day 1

 **Organization**   The way you organize your writing depends on what you are writing about.

A. Makayla is writing about how to set up a new fish tank. Read the two explanations. Write an *X* next to the one that is organized more clearly.

☐ When you set up a fish tank, put plants and gravel in it. Put the fish in. But you have to make sure the tank is clean. The water has to sit for three days before the fish can go in. Use a heater to make the water warmer. My older brother helped me set up my newest fish tank.

☐ It's easy to set up a new fish tank. First, wash your new tank and put gravel in the bottom. Next, pour in water. Add plants, rocks, and caves. Then, put in a heater to warm up the water. Let the water sit for a few days. Finally, add your fish.

B. Write the four order words that were used in the second explanation.

_____ _____ _____ _____

C. Write the form of each of these adjectives that were used in the first explanation. Find and circle the words in the paragraph.

1. new, newer, _____

2. old, _____, oldest

3. _____, cleaner, cleanest

4. warm, _____, warmest

48   **ORGANIZATION**   Daily 6-Trait Writing • EMC 6793 • © Evan-Moor Corp.

Week 5 • Day 2

 Choose the best way to organize your writing to fit your topic and purpose.

A. Read the ways to organize different types of writing. Then read each topic. Write the letter of the best way to organize the topic.

Ways to Organize

a. **Compare and Contrast:** Group things by how they are alike and different.
b. **Tell a Story:** Write a beginning, middle, and ending.
c. **Describe:** Group ideas and details together.
d. **Explain How:** Put steps in the right order.

Topics

How to Clean a Fish Tank _____

The Magic Sea Horse Finds a Home _____

Ocean Animals: The Smallest and the Biggest _____

What's in a Fishpond? _____

B. Choose one of the topics above. If you were going to write about it, which of these graphic organizers would you use to plan your writing? Circle it.

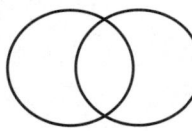   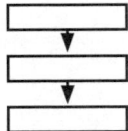   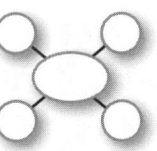

C. Circle the words that end in *est* under "Topics." Then write two sentences using those words.

1. _____

2. _____

Week 5 • Day 3

 Choose the best way to organize your writing.

A. The sentences in this paragraph are out of order. Which would be the best way to reorganize it? Check the box.

> The horn shark and the leopard shark both live off the Pacific Coast. The horn shark is smaller than the leopard shark. The leopard shark has spots that look like a leopard's fur. The horn shark grows up to only 3 feet long. The horn shark was named for the large spines on its fin. The leopard shark grows up to 6 feet.

☐ Group ideas and details together.
☐ Put steps in the right order.
☐ Group things by how they are alike and different.
☐ Write a beginning, middle, and ending.

B. Draw a graphic organizer to help you reorganize the paragraph above. Write the details from the paragraph in your graphic organizer.

Week 5 • Day 4

 Choose the best way to organize your writing.

Choose one of these topics to write about. Then draw a graphic organizer and plan your ideas.

☐ How two sea creatures are alike and different
☐ A description of an octopus
☐ How to make a sand castle

Week 5 • Day 5

Use the ideas in the graphic organizer you created on Day 4 to write a well-organized paragraph.

Be sure to use adjectives that end in *er* or *est* correctly.

Week 1 • Day 1

 **Word Choice** — Strong verbs make your writing come alive! Avoid "tired" verbs, such as *go* and *get*.

A. Read each sentence. Look at the underlined verb. Write three stronger verbs from the box that you could use instead.

Strong Verbs				
climbed	hopped	pranced	sprinted	trotted
dashed	jumped	raced	swooshed	trudged
galloped	leaped	skidded	tramped	tumbled

1. The hikers slowly <u>went</u> up to the top of the hill.

   _____   _____   _____

2. Tina and her horse <u>went</u> around the ring.

   _____   _____   _____

3. The two runners <u>got</u> across the finish line at the same time.

   _____   _____   _____

4. The gymnast <u>got</u> onto the balance beam too quickly and almost fell.

   _____   _____   _____

5. The skier <u>went</u> down the mountain.

   _____   _____   _____

B. Reread the sentences above. Find and circle the words *to*, *too*, and *two*.

Week 1 • Day 2

 **Word Choice** — Use strong, vivid verbs to tell exactly what you mean.

A. Read this news report about a soccer game. Circle the stronger verb in each underlined pair.

Soccer Game Ends in Tie

The Tuckville Tigers <u>battled / played</u> the Harrison Hawks last night in a thrilling soccer match. The Hawks gained the lead when Misha Tamm <u>took / stole</u> the ball and <u>darted / ran</u> downfield. She <u>blasted / kicked</u> the ball into the net. But the Tigers' Dan Beckum scored a goal at the last second. The ball <u>went / sailed</u> over the goalie's head just as the final whistle <u>shrieked / blew</u>.

B. Write two sentences about your favorite sport. Use three verbs from the box, or think of your own, to describe the action.

Strong Verbs					
pass	spin	swing	glide	dribble	race
whack	charge	spring	slide	slam	dive

_____

_____

_____

C. Write *to*, *too*, or *two* in the blanks to finish the sentence.

There were _____ many kids going _____ the game, so we took _____ buses.

Week 1 • Day 3

 **Word Choice** Use adverbs to help make the action in your writing clear and interesting.

Look at the picture. Read the words in the boxes. Combine each adverb with a verb to write four sentences about the picture.

Adverbs	
dizzily	gracefully
boldly	tightly

Verbs	
twirling	zooming
gliding	gripping

1. _____
2. _____
3. _____
4. _____

Week 1 • Day 4

 **Word Choice** — Choose strong verbs and adverbs to make your writing exciting!

If you could be in the Olympics, which sport would you compete in? What are some of the actions or tricks in that sport? How would you perform them? Use the chart below to list your ideas. Use strong verbs and adverbs to describe the action.

My Olympic Sport: _____

Action or Trick	How I Would Do It

Week 1 • Day 5

 Imagine that you have just competed in the Olympics! Write a paragraph telling what happened. Use vivid verbs and adverbs. Be sure to use *to, too,* and *two* correctly.

Week 2 • Day 1

 **Word Choice** Make your writing sparkle! Use colorful adjectives to describe people, places, animals, and things.

A. Read the adjectives in the box. Write two that describe each insect.

Colorful Adjectives				
wiggly	spiky	tiny	squishy	shiny
spotted	hungry	moist	creepy	fuzzy

worm

adjectives: _____
_____

beetle

adjectives: _____
_____

ladybug

adjectives: _____
_____

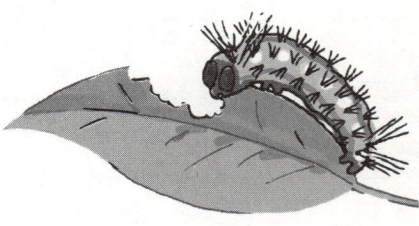

caterpillar

adjectives: _____
_____

B. Write a sentence about one of the bugs. Use two adjectives. Remember to use a comma between them.

_____

_____

58 **WORD CHOICE**   Daily 6-Trait Writing • EMC 6793 • © Evan-Moor Corp.

Week 2 • Day 2

Word Choice

Make your writing sparkle! Use more than one adjective to describe something.

A. Read the thank-you letter Jasmine wrote. Underline the two adjectives that describe each noun in bold. Write the comma between the adjectives.

333 Ladybug Lane
Garden City, KS 67846
January 17, 2009

Dear Aunt Bea,

   Thank you so much for the amber necklace. It is a very special unique **present**. I love its soft golden **color**. I was surprised to see the tiny ancient **insect** inside the amber. I can't believe the amber is millions of years old! Thank you for such a wonderful unusual **gift**.

                    Love from your niece,
                    Jasmine

B. Write a sentence about a special present you have received. Use two colorful adjectives to describe it. Be sure to use a comma between the adjectives.

_____

_____

_____

Week 2 • Day 3

 Make your sentences super! Use colorful adjectives to write longer sentences.

A. Write colorful adjectives to complete the chart. Then put together the words in each row to write five super sentences. The first one is done for you.

	Adjective	Adjective	What?	Did What?	Where?
1	That	tiny	striped	bee	buzzed	around the flowers
2	The		delicate	butterfly	flitted	over the birdbath
3	A	shiny		dragonfly	zoomed	across the pond
4	The			moth	fluttered	past the window
5	An			fly	landed	on my nose

1. That tiny, striped bee buzzed around the flowers.
2. _____
3. _____
4. _____
5. _____

B. Look back at the chart. Write two more super sentences, using any of the words from each column.

1. _____
_____
2. _____
_____

Week 2 • Day 4

 **Word Choice** — Choose just the right adjectives to describe your topic.

Imagine that you are a scientist who has just discovered a new bug! Draw it in detail and label its parts. Then list adjectives to describe it.

My Bug's Name: _____

_____   _____
_____   _____
_____   _____
_____   _____

WORD CHOICE

Imagine that you are a scientist who has discovered a new bug! Write a letter to another scientist, describing your bug in detail.

Be sure to write commas between adjectives.

Week 3 • Day 1

 Use exact nouns in place of weak ones to make your writing stronger.

A. Read each poem. Look at the underlined words. Then answer the questions.

Poem A

Toy Boat

I found my brother's old toy boat,
And played with it today.
I added paper sails to it.
My <u>toy boat</u> flew—hooray!
A captain's <u>boat</u> it became,
And chugged around the bay.
A sailor's <u>boat</u> rescued me,
And carried me away.
An old man's <u>boat</u>, that was next.
I drifted in the sun.
The skipper's <u>boat</u> towed me in,
When my day was done.

Poem B

Toy Boat

I found my brother's old toy boat,
And played with it today.
I added paper sails to it.
My <u>sailboat</u> flew—hooray!
A captain's <u>ferry</u> it became,
And chugged around the bay.
A sailor's <u>lifeboat</u> rescued me,
And carried me away.
An old man's <u>rowboat</u>, that was next.
I drifted in the sun.
The skipper's <u>tugboat</u> towed me in,
When my day was done.

1. Which poem uses exact nouns? _____

2. Which exact nouns help the reader see what the speaker imagines while playing with the toy boat?

_____

B. Add an apostrophe and *s* to each word to make a possessive noun.

brother____   captain____   sailor____   man____   skipper____

Week 3 • Day 2

 **Word Choice** — Use exact nouns instead of weak ones.

A. Read the report. Write an exact noun for *boat* to complete each sentence. Use the words in the box.

Exact Nouns		
canoes	oil tankers	steamships
cruise ships	sailing ships	submarines

Can you imagine living without boats? For hundreds of years, Native Americans made _____ in order to trade with faraway tribes. In 1492, Columbus and his crew traveled to America in _____ _____. Hundreds of years later, _____ chugged across the ocean, bringing people to America.

Today, thousands of _____ carry oil all over the world. Some people work under the ocean on _____. Others enjoy vacations on large _____. Boats have always helped us get from one place to another.

B. Show who or what owns these things. Use the word under each line to write a possessive noun. Be sure to use an apostrophe and *s*.

a _____ canoe   the _____ journey
   (child)   (explorer)

a _____ oars   the _____ crew
   (boat)   (ship)

Week 3 • Day 3

 **Word Choice** Use exact nouns to make your writing more interesting.

Write exact nouns to finish the paragraphs about a family's trip. Use nouns that will make your story fun to read.

My First Train Ride

Last summer, Mom had a great idea. "Let's visit your aunt in _____ (place) for a week," she bubbled. Mom bought four tickets for a train called the _____ (name) _____. She said it would be a long, easy ride—much better than driving in our old _____ (kind of car).

Once we boarded the train, I looked around. There were many _____ (people) and _____ (people). I wondered where they were all going.

For the first hour, I watched everything speed past the window. As the train chugged along, I saw some _____ (animals) in the fields. Then we passed through the mountains, and I saw _____ (birds).

A woman pushed a snack cart down the aisle, and I bought _____ (snack) to eat later. Then I stretched out on the seat and read _____ (book title) until we arrived at our aunt's town.

Week 3 • Day 4

 **Word Choice** — Use exact nouns to make your writing more interesting.

Plan a poem about taking a trip. Choose a place to go. How will you get there? Who will go with you? Write your ideas and details below. List exact nouns that you might use in your poem.

My Trip

1. I am going to travel to _____

2. I will travel by _____
   _____

3. These people or pets are going with me:
   _____   _____
   _____   _____

4. On the way, we'll see _____
   _____

5. When we get there, we will _____
   _____

Week 3 • Day 5

 Write a poem about taking a trip, using exact nouns. Be sure to write singular possessive nouns correctly.

Week 4 • Day 1

 **Word Choice** — Use similes to dress up your writing. A simile makes a comparison using the words *like* or *as*.

A. Circle the two things that are compared in each simile below.

1. The snow fell as quietly as a feather.

2. The girls on the trampoline looked like kangaroos.

3. The rain on the roof pounded like drums in a marching band.

4. The hot chocolate felt like a volcano erupting on my tongue.

5. The train sounded like a thunderstorm on its way through town.

6. The kids on the playground were as loud as monkeys.

B. Finish the similes.

1. The kitten's eyes were as bright as _____.

2. The bird was as quick as _____.

3. Spring is like _____.

C. Read each sentence. Write the pronoun that replaces the underlined noun.

1. Brandon washed <u>Brandon's</u> hands. _____

2. Annie finished <u>Annie's</u> homework. _____

3. The students listened to <u>the students'</u> teacher. _____

Week 4 • Day 2

 **Word Choice** — Use metaphors to dress up your writing. A metaphor describes something by comparing it to something very different. It does not use *like* or *as*.

A. Read each metaphor. Then complete the sentence to tell what is being compared. Mark an *X* by the phrase that tells why the two words are being compared.

1. *The music is the heartbeat of the people.*

   Music is compared to a _____ because they

   _____ are both loud.

   _____ both have a beat.

   _____ are both necessary to stay alive.

2. *The candle became the sun, lighting the dark world.*

   A candle is compared to the _____ because they

   _____ are both in the sky.

   _____ both burn at night.

   _____ both light the darkness.

3. *The children's voices were bells ringing through the streets.*

   The voices are compared to _____ because they

   _____ sound musical.

   _____ are silent.

   _____ make the same sound over and over.

B. What could you compare to twinkling stars? Write a sentence containing a metaphor that compares something to stars.

_____

Week 4 • Day 3

Similes and metaphors make your writing sparkle.

A. Read the poem. Fill in a word to complete each metaphor.

My Sister Is…

A lion when she gets mad at me,
A puppy when she's asleep in her bed,
A _____ when she gobbles down her food,
And a _____ when she stands on her head.
She's a _____ when she runs for the bus,
A _____ when she whistles and sings.
She's a _____ when she wants to be lazy.
My sister is all of these things!

B. Write the missing possessive pronouns in this paragraph. Then underline the similes and metaphors.

Possessive Pronouns
its   our   his   my

Yesterday, my brother Tito let me fly _____ kite. We went to the beach near _____ home to fly it. But the wind was howling like a dog. We could barely hold onto the string. Tito was a fisherman, fighting to reel in the kite. I grabbed hold of _____ brother, trying to keep him on the ground. Suddenly, the kite was a jet taking us for a ride! We flew along like seagulls skimming the ocean. Finally, the wind stopped howling. It had lost _____ voice.

Week 4 • Day 4

 **Word Choice** — When you write a poem, use similes and metaphors to communicate your ideas.

Plan a poem that describes yourself, a friend, or a member of your family. List their qualities. Write similes or metaphors to describe the qualities.

Person: _____

Quality	Simile or Metaphor
Examples:	
funny	as funny as a pig on rollerskates
smart	like Albert Einstein
1.	
2.	
3.	
4.	
5.	
6.	

WORD CHOICE

Week 4 • Day 5

 **Word Choice** — Write a poem with metaphors or similes to describe yourself or someone you know.

Be sure to use possessive pronouns correctly.

Week 5 • Day 1

 Use strong verbs to get your reader's attention.

A. Read the news article. Look at the pairs of verbs under the lines. Write the one in each pair that is more attention-getting.

Dog Saves Owner

On March 23, 2007, something amazing happened in Calvert, Maryland. Toby, a two-year-old golden retriever, _____ his owner _____ to
(saw / discovered)   (trying / struggling)
breathe. Debbie Parkhurst had a piece of apple lodged in her throat, and she was choking. Toby _____
(pushed / knocked)
her to the ground. Then he _____ on her
(jumped / got)
chest until he _____ the apple to
(forced / got)
_____ out. Toby _____ his
(come / pop)   (rescued / helped)
owner! For his efforts, Toby _____ the Dog
(received / got)
of the Year award.

B. When were you born? Write the date to finish the sentence. Then write the date of a classmate's birthday. Be sure to write the commas in the proper places.

On _____ I was born.

On _____ was born.

Week 5 • Day 2

 **Word Choice** Use colorful adjectives and strong adverbs to get your reader's attention.

A. Read the article. Write the missing commas in the first sentence. Then write adjectives and adverbs from the box to complete the article.

Adjectives and Adverbs					
gently	terrified	carefully	huge	frightened	suddenly

An Unusual Gorilla

On August 16 1996 there was an accident at the Brookfield Zoo in Chicago. A three-year-old boy fell _____ into the gorilla exhibit. The little boy's _____ mother called for help.

Before anyone else could get there, a gorilla named Binti Jua came to the rescue. She picked up the hurt boy and _____ held him to her chest.

A _____ male gorilla came toward them. But when Binti Jua growled, the big gorilla backed away. She carried the boy to the door that her keepers always used and _____ placed him there. The boy was saved!

B. Write two sentences telling what you think about Binti Jua. Use colorful adjectives and adverbs.

_____

_____

Week 5 • Day 3

 **Word Choice** — Use exact nouns and phrases to get your reader's attention.

Read this movie review about *Balto*. Did the writer get your attention? Cross out the words in bold and write more exact nouns and phrases above them. Use the words in the box.

Exact Nouns and Phrases		
sick children	a life-saving medicine	Siberian husky
cartoon movie	serious disease called diphtheria	a grizzly bear

A Movie That Will Give You Chills

Can you imagine traveling hundreds of miles through the freezing snow? This actually happened in Alaska in 1925, and the amazing story is told in the **film** *Balto*.

Balto, a **dog**, must run a sled race—a race against time. Children in Nome, Alaska, are suffering from a **sickness** and need **help**. Balto leads the sled dog team carrying the medicine to Nome.

This is an action-packed movie that keeps you in your seat. First, Balto is attacked by **an animal**. Then, the team gets lost. Will they make it in time? Will Balto rescue the **people** of Nome? Watch *Balto* and find out!

Week 5 • Day 4

 **Word Choice** — Get your reader's attention with the words you choose.

A. Plan a movie review. Choose a movie you've seen and would like to write about. Then write exact nouns and phrases, colorful adjectives, and strong verbs and adverbs that tell about the movie.

Movie Title:

Exact Nouns and Phrases:

Strong Verbs:

Colorful Adjectives:

Strong Adverbs:

B. Write the date you saw the movie. If you don't remember, just guess.

_____

Week 5 • Day 5

Write a movie review. Use exact nouns and phrases, colorful adjectives, strong verbs, and strong adverbs.

In one sentence, include the date that you saw the movie. Be sure to write the commas in the proper places.

Week 1 • Day 1

 **Sentence Fluency** — Begin your sentences in different ways to make your writing more interesting.

A. Read each student's report. Circle the first word of each sentence. Then draw a star by the report that has more sentences that begin in different ways.

Saturn: The Ringed Planet
by Rina

Saturn is the second-largest planet in our solar system. It was seen for the first time in 1610. A scientist saw rings around it. Its rings are made of ice and rock. It has over fifty moons! Its farthest moon is named Fornjot.

Pluto: Not a Planet Anymore
by Vince

Poor little Pluto! It used to be the ninth planet in our solar system. Then, in 2006, scientists had a meeting about Pluto's size. They took a vote. Now, little Pluto is no longer a true planet. Instead, it is known as a dwarf planet.

B. Rewrite one of the sentences from Rina's report so that it begins differently.

_____

_____

C. Find the word *seen* in Rina's report. Write the helping word that comes before it.

_____ seen

Week 1 • Day 2

 Make your writing more interesting by varying the length of your sentences. Make some of them long, and some of them short.

A. Read this paragraph. Then read the pairs of sentences in the box. Write the sentence from each pair that sounds best in the paragraph.

Have you ever seen a light streak through the night sky? That light you saw is often called a "shooting star." ① _____

It is a tiny bit of dust or rock falling very quickly toward Earth. As it falls, the rock burns. ② _____
_____

The scientific name for the object is "meteor."

---

① But it's not really a star at all.

But it actually has nothing to do with stars at all!

② What we see is the trail of flames shooting across the sky.

It leaves a trail of flames.

B. Read each sentence. Use proofreading marks to correct the errors with *saw* and *seen*.

1. I seen a meteor shower three years ago.

2. My dad has saw several meteor showers.

3. A meteor shower was saw in Norway last month.

Week 1 • Day 3

 **Sentence Fluency:** Use a variety of sentence types to make your writing more interesting.

A. Read this journal entry. Use a straight line to underline each question. Use a wavy line to underline each exclamation.

> October 24, 2008
>
> I just saw a new object in the sky! What could it be? I looked online to find out. It turns out that someone in Spain has seen it. People in New Mexico and Minnesota have seen it, too. I found out it is a comet named Comet Holmes. How many more nights will I be able to see it? No one knows!

B. Write two different types of sentences about something you have seen in the sky. It can be real or made up.

_____

_____

C. Read each sentence. Does it need a helping verb to complete it? If so, write the helping verb. If not, write an *X*.

1. Britta _____ saw a huge building with a round roof.

2. Her mother _____ seen it, too.

3. Dad said, "I _____ seen that before. There is a giant telescope in there."

Week 1 • Day 4

 Vary your sentences to make your writing more interesting.

Imagine that you are a scientist who watches the sky at night. You have just seen something new and exciting! Write notes in your logbook about what you saw. Be sure to include plenty of details!

LOGBOOK Date: _____

_____
_____
_____
_____
_____
_____
_____
_____
_____
_____
_____
_____
_____
_____
_____
_____

Week 1 • Day 5

Imagine that you are a scientist who saw something amazing in the night sky. Write a science article describing what you saw. Use a variety of sentence beginnings, lengths, and types.

Be sure to use *saw* and *seen* correctly.

Week 2 • Day 1

 Combine choppy sentences to make your writing sound smoother. Use a comma and the joining words *and, but,* and *or.*

A. Read these paragraphs. Write an *X* next to the one that has too many short, choppy sentences.

☐ I love nature and the outdoors. I like helping my dad rake the yard, but I like planting new flowers more! I even enjoy reading about rain forests, and I like watching TV shows about nature. Maybe someday I will create gardens for people, or I will help save a rain forest.

☐ I like pets. They're what I like most. I have two cats. I also have a dog. I wish I had an iguana. I even like to read books about pets. Someday, I will take care of more animals. I want to be a vet. Then I could always be around pets.

B. Read each pair of sentences. Then rewrite them as one sentence by using a comma and the joining word in parentheses.

1. I am a dancer. You are a skater. *(and)*

   _____

2. Tori knows how to swim. She doesn't like it. *(but)*

   _____

3. Jamal will be a doctor. He will be a teacher. *(or)*

   _____

SENTENCE FLUENCY

Week 2 • Day 2

 **Sentence Fluency** — You can combine short, choppy sentences by joining the subjects of two similar sentences.

A. Read each pair of sentences. Combine their subjects to create one sentence.

1. My mom is a nurse. My grandma is a nurse.

   _____

2. My dad teaches music. My uncle teaches music.

   _____

B. Read the paragraph. Underline two pairs of sentences that could be combined. Then combine the sentences in each pair to make longer sentences. Write the new sentences.

   Yesterday was Career Day at our school. Judge Patel came to talk. Officer Cortez came to talk. We learned about laws and courts. Then a bus driver talked about her job. A doctor talked about his job. They both said it is their job to make people safe.

1. _____

   _____

2. _____

   _____

Week 2 • Day 3

 One way to combine short, choppy sentences is to join the predicates of similar sentences.

A. Read each pair of sentences. Combine their predicates to create one sentence.

1. A reporter asks questions. A reporter writes about the answers.

   _____

2. Mr. Flay is a reporter. He writes for the newspaper.

   _____

B. Read this paragraph. Underline the two pairs of sentences that can be combined. Rewrite each pair as one sentence.

> Being a TV weather forecaster would be fun. A forecaster predicts the temperature. A forecaster warns about storms. I think I would be good at these things. I like looking at weather maps. I like studying the clouds in the sky. It might be hard work but I enjoy helping people.

1. _____

   _____

2. _____

   _____

C. Reread the paragraph above. Find the compound sentence that needs a comma. Insert the comma and circle the joining word.

Week 2 • Day 4

 **Sentence Fluency** Combine sentences in different ways to make your writing flow smoothly.

A. If you could choose between any of the careers in the box below, which would you pick? Why? Use the chart to jot down your ideas.

- In the **Pros** column, write what you *would like* about the career.
- In the **Cons** column, write what you *would not like* about the career.

Careers

| doctor | astronaut | weather forecaster |
| principal | zookeeper | ballet dancer |

Career: _____

Pros	Cons

B. Combine a pro and a con from your chart to write a compound sentence about the career you chose.

_____

_____

Week 2 • Day 5

Write a paragraph about a career you would like to have. Combine short sentences to make your writing flow.

Be sure to use a comma and a joining word in compound sentences.

Week 3 • Day 1

 A run-on sentence is two sentences joined together. Be sure to fix run-on sentences by breaking them up correctly.

A. Read each sentence. If it is a run-on sentence, use proofreading marks to insert the correct end mark and capitalize the first word in the second sentence.

1. Have you seen my dollar it is missing.

2. It is in your wallet.

3. I thought I dropped it, here it is.

4. You should keep your wallet in a safe place.

5. Where will it be safe I always lose things!

B. Read the paragraph. Find the run-on sentences. Fix each one by deleting the comma and adding a period, a question mark, or an exclamation point.

   Have you ever bought anything at the Save Big Store? I got five dollars for my birthday, I bought a few packs of baseball cards there. I also received a gift card I didn't know what to do with it. My dad said I could spend it at the Save Big Store, too! It is just like using cash. What did I do, I went right back to the store. I bought more baseball cards!

Week 3 • Day 2

 Avoid long, rambling sentences with too many *ands* or *buts*. Fix a rambling sentence by breaking it into smaller sentences.

A. Read these paragraphs about coin collecting. Underline the rambling sentences. Circle the words *and* and *but* in each one.

Coin Collecting

Coin collecting is a great hobby because there are many different coins to collect from other countries. I have coins from Canada and I have a lot from the United States but I want more coins from Mexico, and I would like some coins from Europe.

Most coins show the name of the country they come from and they also show how much the coin is worth, but not all coins show the year they were made, but you can still collect those. I have coins that have pictures of people on them, and I also have coins that have pictures of animals or buildings and some coins don't have pictures on them at all.

B. Choose one of the rambling sentences from above. Rewrite it by breaking the sentence into smaller sentences.

_____
_____
_____
_____

Week 3 • Day 3

Sentence Fluency — Watch out for run-on and rambling sentences! Correct them by breaking them into smaller sentences.

A. Read this report. Find the run-on sentences and underline them. Find the rambling sentence and underline it twice.

Wampum

Wampum was a form of money used by many Native Americans, it was also used by people living in the colonies. Wampum was made from shells carved into beads. The beads were made into belts, the belts were very valuable. People traded wampum for furs, and they used it to send messages and they told stories with it. Today, you can see wampum in museums.

B. Rewrite the paragraph above. Break the run-on and rambling sentences into smaller sentences. Be sure to use commas correctly.

_____
_____
_____
_____
_____
_____
_____

Week 3 • Day 4

 Avoid writing run-on and rambling sentences.

Imagine that you won a million dollars! What would you do with the money? Answer the questions in the web.

Spend?
What would you buy?

Save?
How much would you save? What for?

Give?
How much would you give away? To whom?

SENTENCE FLUENCY

Week 3 • Day 5

 Write a paragraph about what you would do if you won a million dollars! Be sure to avoid writing run-on and rambling sentences. Use commas and end punctuation correctly.

Week 4 • Day 1

 **Sentence Fluency** — You can use the joining words *so, because,* and *if* to combine sentences.

A. Circle the joining word in each sentence. Underline the two smaller sentences that were combined.

> **Joining Words**
> so   because   if

1. Roger decided to learn the trumpet so he could play in the band.

2. Shana likes the drums because they are loud.

3. I will play the tuba if you help me carry it!

B. Read each pair of sentences. Choose the best joining word to combine the sentences into one sentence. Then write the new sentence.

1. I can't go to music class. I am sick.
   _____
   _____

2. Jordan sings quietly. He doesn't wake the baby.
   _____
   _____

3. I would play the flute better. I would practice more.
   _____
   _____

Week 4 • Day 2

 You can use the joining words *before, after, once, when,* and *while* to combine sentences that tell when something happened.

A. Read each sentence. Underline the joining word. Circle the comma if there is one.

1. When my sister plays her violin, I put my hands over my ears.

2. She will get better once she has more practice.

3. After Kysha learns to play the piano, she wants to try the guitar.

4. The choir practices singing while the band members tune their instruments.

B. Read each pair of sentences. Then combine the sentences, beginning with the given joining word.

1. The concert started. Mr. Bell thanked his students.

   Before _____

   _____

2. The concert ended. The students took a bow.

   When _____

   _____

3. The band packed up. The parents got ready for the party.

   While _____

   _____

Week 4 • Day 3

 **Sentence Fluency** Use a joining word to combine two ideas into one sentence.

Read this paragraph. Underline the three pairs of sentences that can be combined. Then write them as combined sentences on the lines. Use the joining words in the box.

Joining Words
after   because   while

I love listening to the Chipmunks. They are my favorite group. My whole family likes them. Sometimes it is hard to find music that everyone likes. We used to argue about what to listen to in the car. We got the Chipmunks CD. All of us were happy. My brother and I sing the songs. My parents drive in peace.

1. _____

2. _____

3. _____

SENTENCE FLUENCY

Week 4 • Day 4

 **Sentence Fluency** Use a joining word to combine two ideas into one sentence.

Plan a description about your favorite singer, musician, or band. Answer the questions to help you.

1. Who is your favorite musical performer?
   _____

2. What are your favorite songs by that performer?
   _____

3. Why do you like the performer? Use the word *because* in your answer.
   _____
   _____

4. When do you listen to the performer? Use the words *after, before, when,* or *while* in your answer.
   _____
   _____

5. What would you do if you met the performer? Use the word *if* in your answer.
   _____
   _____
   _____

Week 4 • Day 5

Sentence Fluency

Describe your favorite singer, musician, or band. Use joining words such as *after, because, before, if, when,* or *while.*

If you begin a sentence with a joining word, write a comma between the two ideas in the sentence.

Week 5 • Day 1

 Make your paragraph flow by using joining words to combine ideas.

A. Choose the best joining word from the box to connect the ideas in each sentence. Write it on the line. Add commas where needed.

Joining Words				
if	because	but	and	while

Alexander Graham Bell was an inventor _____ he started out as a teacher of deaf students. _____ there is one thing he is best known for inventing it is the telephone. _____ working on his invention Bell spoke the first words on the telephone. He said to his helper, "Mr. Watson, come here." Later, he started the Bell Telephone Company _____ everyone wanted a telephone. Bell lived until he was 75 years old _____ he never stopped working.

B. Some past tense verbs do not have *ed* at the end. Read each sentence. Circle the past tense verb that is incorrect. Then write the correct verb on the line.

1. Bell speaked to Mr. Watson using the telephone. _____

2. The telephone maked Bell famous. _____

3. He also teached deaf students. _____

Week 5 • Day 2

 Fix run-on and rambling sentences to make your paragraph flow better.

A. Read the paragraph. Fix each incorrect past tense verb. Then find and underline one run-on and one rambling sentence.

You see them in offices, schools, and homes. They're stick-on notes! These handy little notes were invented by two people named Arthur Fry and Spencer Silver. They worked for the 3M Company. Silver was a scientist, he invented a glue that wasn't very sticky, nobody knowed what to do with it. Fry was a scientist who invented new products for the 3M Company. He also singed in a choir. He used slips of paper to mark his choir book, but the papers fell out, and that made Arthur angry, and he used Silver's glue to create stick-on notes.

B. Choose one of the sentences you underlined above. Break it into smaller sentences that flow together well. Write the sentences below.

_____
_____
_____
_____

Week 5 • Day 3

 A smooth paragraph has sentences that begin in different ways. It has long and short sentences, and it has a mix of statements, questions, and exclamations.

Read Howie's story about meeting an inventor. Then rewrite the story so it flows more smoothly.

Meeting Mary Anderson

It was 1903. I was in a car. It was raining. I couldn't see where I was going. I stopped the car. I saw a woman. She was Mary Anderson. She said she could help. She put a long rubber blade on my windshield. It wiped the rain right off. I could see again. I'm glad I met the inventor of the windshield wiper!

Week 5 • Day 4

 A smooth paragraph has sentences and ideas that flow.

Imagine that you could travel back in time and meet an inventor. Imagine the inventor showed you his or her invention! Answer the questions, using complete sentences.

1. Who was the inventor?
   _____

2. What did the inventor invent?
   _____

3. Why was the invention important?
   _____
   _____

4. What year or place did you travel back to in order to meet the inventor?
   _____

5. What else happened when you met the inventor?
   _____
   _____
   _____

Week 5 • Day 5

 Write a story about going back in time and meeting an inventor. Make your story flow smoothly from one sentence to the next.

Be sure to use the correct past tense form of verbs.

Week 1 • Day 1

 **Voice** — Some writing has a playful voice. It makes the writing fun to read.

A. Read the article below. Then answer the question.

The Mummy Always Wins

You are a scientist digging in a mummy's tomb. You find treasures of gold and gems. They are the Egyptian king's favorite belongings. What's this? It looks like...can it be? Yes, it's a checkers game!

Scientists found 3,000-year-old checkers sets among the treasures buried with mummies. Why did ancient kings play checkers? The game of checkers is played with pieces called "men." Both players try to capture the other side's men, like two armies. Maybe that's why kings enjoyed playing it. If you meet a mummy, you should ask him to play!

Which of these things are in the article? Mark an *X*.

____ a surprise   ____ a funny title   ____ a silly ending

B. Draw a line under the sentences that fit the voice of the article.

1. How would you like to play checkers with a mummy?

2. Wake up, mummy, it's your turn!

3. Ancient Egyptian kings played checkers.

C. Circle the contractions in the article. Write them below.

1. _____   2. _____   3. _____

Week 1 • Day 2

 **Voice** — Some writing has a formal, serious-sounding voice.

A. Read Austin's story. Think about the voice he used. Underline words or phrases that sound formal.

   Several years ago, when I was a young child, my father used to take me along on his fishing trips. I was too small to hold a real fishing rod, so I would pretend to fish with a stick. I hoped that someday I would receive a real rod.

   Last year, my father and I went shopping for Christmas presents for my younger brother. In the toy store, I saw a toy fishing rod. "You should get Dylan that," I suggested. "When I was his age, I loved pretending to fish with you."

   "You remember?" inquired my father, looking pleased.

   That Christmas, two rods sat carefully placed under the tree. One was the toy rod for Dylan, and the other was a real rod for me. The tag on it read, "We'll go fishing this spring. Now you won't have to pretend. Love, Dad."

B. Write two sentences about a special memory you have. Use a serious voice to show how the event was important to you.

_____

_____

_____

104 VOICE   Daily 6-Trait Writing • EMC 6793 • © Evan-Moor Corp.

Week 1 • Day 3

 **Voice** Some writing has a voice that shows excitement!

A. Read Roger's letter. Fix the incorrectly written contractions.

> Dear Grandma,
>   I had to thank you right away for the incredible birthday gift! I didnt' expect to get my very own video game system. Its the greatest present ever! Have you ever played it? If not, Ill tell you about it. You hold the controller and choose a sport to play, like baseball. Then you stand in front of the TV and get ready to react quickly. When you see the ball on the screen, you immediately swing at it. Its' so much fun! I can't wait till the next time you visit. Il'l teach you how to play.
>   Love,
>   Roger

B. How did Roger show excitement in his writing? Underline two sentences that show strong feelings. Then circle:
- two strong adjectives
- two strong adverbs
- three punctuation marks that show excitement

C. Write two sentences about an exciting game you like to play. Use a voice that shows your excitement.

_____

_____

Week 1 • Day 4

 **Voice** You can write in a funny, serious, or exciting voice.

Think about your favorite game or toy. If you were going to write about it, what would you say? Answer the questions.

1. If you were allowed to keep only one toy, what would it be?
   _____

2. How would you describe the toy?
   _____
   _____

3. Why would you choose this toy to write about?
   _____
   _____

4. Did someone give it to you? Who? When?
   _____
   _____

5. Why is this toy special?
   _____
   _____

6. What voice would you use to write about your toy? Mark an *X*.
   ☐ Serious   ☐ Exciting   ☐ Funny

Week 1 • Day 5

 Write about your favorite game or toy. Use a serious, funny, or exciting voice.

Be sure to spell contractions correctly.

Week 2 • Day 1

 **Voice** You can use formal or informal language when you write.

A. Read the e-mail message and the picture caption. They have similar purposes, but one uses *informal language* and the other uses *formal language*. Write the style of language and the audience for each one.

E-mail

Hi, Uncle Ravi!
   Here's a pic of me last Fri. at the school art show. I made this mask out of paper, paste, and paint. Wish you could come to L.A. to see it!
Hugs, Chitra

Purpose: to tell about a mask

Style:

_____

Audience:

_____

Picture Caption

   The wooden dancer's mask in this picture was created in the nineteenth century. It was made by an unknown Native American artist of the Northwest Coast.

Purpose: to tell about a mask

Style:

_____

Audience:

_____

B. Circle the quotation marks and underline the speaker's words.

   Our museum guide said, "This mask is called a raven mask. It was used by the Nakwoktak tribe."

Week 2 • Day 2

 **Voice** Use a formal voice when you write a report.

A. Read Lila's school report about her trip to a museum.

    My favorite work at the museum is an ancient statue of Athena, the Greek goddess of war and wisdom. The statue shows only her head and shoulders. Her eyes are blank, and she has short hair. She is wearing loose robes and a necklace of snakes.

_____

_____

_____

B. Read the sentences below. Which ones use the same language as Lila's report? Use them to write another paragraph above for the report.

The snakes are freaky looking.
Athena is wearing a war helmet, but she does not look angry.
Maybe she is thinking about how serious war is.
You can't see her eyes, and that's totally weird.
Without eyes, you have to guess what she feels.
What is up with that goofy helmet?

C. Write what you think Lila would tell a friend about the statue. Be sure to put quotation marks around her words.

   <u>Lila would say,</u>_____

_____

© Evan-Moor Corp. • EMC 6793 • Daily 6-Trait Writing   VOICE 109

Week 2 • Day 3

 **Voice** Use the right voice throughout your writing.

A. Read the postcard and newspaper article. Circle the sentences that do not stick to the right voice.

Postcard (informal voice)

Hi Jake,

My class went to see this play called "The Sound of Music." It was kind of weird that the characters were always singing and dancing. The musical, based on a true story, follows the courageous Von Trapp family through difficult times. A girl in my class was in it. This made the show quite special for the students!

Brian

News Article (formal voice)

On March 2, 2009, Ms. Murray's third-grade class attended "The Sound of Music" at Forest Theater. It's a musical about a big family trying to escape some bad guys. The cast included one of the students' classmates. That was pretty cool.

B. Rewrite the postcard or the newspaper article so that all of the sentences are in the right voice.

_____
_____
_____
_____

Week 2 • Day 4

 **Voice** — Use formal or informal language in your writing.

Interview a partner about something interesting he or she has done or seen.

1. What did you do or see?
   _____
   _____
   _____

2. When did this happen?
   _____

3. Where did it happen?
   _____

4. Whom did you go with or see?
   _____
   _____

5. Why was this so interesting or special? Write your partner's exact words.
   _____
   _____
   _____
   _____

Week 2 • Day 5

 **Voice**

Using the interview from Day 4, write a newspaper article about something interesting that your partner has done or seen.

Be sure to use quotation marks around your partner's exact words.

Week 3 • Day 1

 **Voice** — A mood makes you feel a certain way. You can create a mood with strong verbs and adjectives.

A. In China, people write rhymes to mark the New Year. Read the rhymes below. Write the word from the box that describes the mood of each rhyme.

1. Colorful dragons and lions, oh my!
   Thrill us as they go parading by.

   Mood: _____

Moods	
cheerful	thrilling
loving	frightening

2. Exploding firecrackers—*boom, bang, pop!*
   Scared babies cry for the noises to stop.

   Mood: _____

3. I give these good-luck oranges to you.
   They're sweet and special, and you are, too.

   Mood: _____

4. The New Year brings another spring;
   Bright flowers bloom, and baby birds sing.

   Mood: _____

B. In each poem above, underline a verb or an adjective that helps create the mood.

C. The first word in every line of a poem should begin with a capital letter. Circle the capital letter at the beginning of each line.

© Evan-Moor Corp. • EMC 6793 • *Daily 6-Trait Writing*   **VOICE** 113

Week 3 • Day 2

 **Voice** — The mood of your writing should match your topic.

A. Padma's family comes from India. Read her cinquain about Diwali, a holiday observed by her family. Write a word to describe the mood of the poem. Then underline the words that create that mood.

> Lamps
> Tiny, clay
> Glowing, flickering, shining
> Give us peaceful light
> Flames
> **Mood:** _____

B. Help Padma finish another poem. Use words from the boxes to give the poem a **joyful** mood. Be sure to capitalize the first word in each line.

Adjectives	Verbs
dangerous joyous	crying sharing
colorful sweet	feasting sleeping
foolish	hoping

Diwali

_____ , _____
(adjective)   (adjective)

_____ , _____ , _____
(verb)   (verb)   (verb)

Five days with family—
Festival

114 VOICE   Daily 6-Trait Writing • EMC 6793 • © Evan-Moor Corp.

Week 3 • Day 3

 **Voice** — Create a mood with words.

A. Read this diamonte about a local jazz music festival. Fix the words that should have capital letters. Then answer the questions.

Music
loud, crazy
singing, dancing, playing
Saxophones, trumpets, curtain, end
Stopping, closing, leaving
empty, still
silence

1. What is the mood at the beginning of the poem? _____

2. What are two words that create this mood?
   _____

3. What is the mood at the end of the poem? _____

4. What are two words that create this mood?
   _____

B. Write three sentences about a festival, fair, or carnival that takes place in your area. Use one of the moods in the poem above, or create your own mood.

_____
_____
_____

Week 3 • Day 4

 **Voice** — When you write a poem, choose your words carefully to create the right mood.

Think about a holiday or celebration your family observes. Use the chart to plan a cinquain about it. Remember that a cinquain does not have to rhyme. The five lines are organized like this:

Line 1: One word that names the subject
Line 2: Two adjectives that describe the subject
Line 3: Three strong verbs ending with *ing* about the subject
Line 4: A four-word phrase that describes a feeling about the subject
Line 5: One word that renames the subject

Line 1

+

Line 2

+

Line 3

+

Line 4

+

Line 5

Week 3 • Day 5

 **Voice** Write a cinquain about a celebration or holiday you observe. Be sure to capitalize the first word in every line of your poem.

Week 4 • Day 1

 **Voice** — Every story has a point of view, or whose side the story is told from.

A. Read what each character from "Goldilocks and the Three Bears" might say if he or she were telling the story. Write the name of the character whose point of view it is.

> **Characters**
> Goldilocks   Papa Bear   Mama Bear   Baby Bear

1. It was a fine morning. Papa agreed, so after I made the porridge, we left it to cool and took Baby out for a walk.

   Point of view: _____

2. Such a cute little cottage! No one answered when I knocked. I discovered that the door wasn't locked, so I went inside.

   Point of view: _____

3. I cried, "Hey, what's going on here?" My little chair had been smashed to pieces! I did NOT like that.

   Point of view: _____

4. After we found the broken chair and empty bowl, I growled to Mama and Baby, "Stay here while I check the bedroom!"

   Point of view: _____

B. Read the words below. Circle the prefixes *un* and *dis*. Then find the base words in Activity A and underline them.

   unlocked   disagreed   unbroken   dislike

Week 4 • Day 2

 **Voice** — A story can be told from different points of view. Your point of view affects the voice you use when you write.

A. Read the story. Then read the possible endings. Choose the one that is from the same point of view. Write it to finish the story.

The Emperor's New Clothes

One day, two merchants claimed they could make me the finest suit from the very best cloth. However, they said the cloth could not be seen by anyone who is unfit for his job. This made me a little uncertain. I'm not a fool, so I sent my officials to see it first. That was a big mistake.

My officials couldn't see the cloth, but they didn't want to be seen as unfit. So they told me how beautiful it was! How could I say that I, the Emperor, couldn't see the cloth? I should have distrusted those merchants. But I paraded out of the palace without a stitch on. No one said a word until a boy cried, "He's not wearing any clothes!"

_____

_____

Possible Endings
We fooled that old emperor. What an idiot!
Now we are in trouble! We told the emperor we could see the cloth.
What could I do? I just held my head up high and walked on.

B. Write the words from the story that match each meaning.

not fit _____   not certain _____

not trusted _____

Week 4 • Day 3

 **Voice** — A story can be told from an outside narrator's point of view.

A. Read these introductions to "The Tortoise and the Hare."
   Mark the one with the point of view of an outside *narrator*.

   ☐ That was the worst day of my life. I can't believe I let that slowpoke beat me!

   ☐ Let me tell you about the time I taught Hare a lesson.

   ☐ One day, Hare was poking fun at Tortoise, which was his favorite thing to do.

B. Write an ending for the story. Be sure to use the same point of view.

The Tortoise and the Hare

"You're so slow!" Hare sniffed. "How do you get anywhere with those short legs?"

"I can get anywhere sooner than you think," replied Tortoise calmly. "How about a race?"

"Sure, Slowpoke, I'll race you!" Hare laughed.

The race began. Tortoise slowly and steadily made his way. But Hare thought he'd show Tortoise. He lay down and took a nap. Tortoise kept on. He passed the sleeping Hare. Too late, Hare awoke and ran as fast as he could.

_____
_____
_____
_____
_____

Week 4 • Day 4

 **Voice** Write from different points of view.

A. Think about the story "The Tortoise and the Hare."
How would each character tell the story from his point of view?
Fill in the chart with your ideas.

The Tortoise and the Hare

The Tortoise's Point of View	The Hare's Point of View

B. Think of words with the prefixes *un-* and *dis-*. Which ones could you use in your story?

Examples: disappear, unhappy

_____

_____

Week 4 • Day 5

Voice

Rewrite the story of "The Tortoise and the Hare." Tell it from the point of view of one of the characters.

Try to use a word with the prefix *un-* or *dis-*.

_____
_____
_____
_____
_____
_____
_____
_____
_____
_____
_____
_____
_____
_____
_____
_____
_____
_____
_____
_____

Week 5 • Day 1

 **Voice** Use your unique voice to show your reader how you feel.

Read the stories by Tam and Le. Then answer the questions.

Tam's Story

The first time I went on a roller coaster was with Le. We climbed in and sat back as the safety bar was closed into place. It was kind of scary. I hoped the bar would stay locked. Then I heard a bell, and the coaster started. We were off!

Le's Story

I remember every minute of my first roller coaster ride! I felt my legs wobble as Tam and I climbed aboard. Click! The safety bar closed across us. I gave it a shake. "Just making sure," I told him. I couldn't wait to be flying down the hills! Somewhere a bell sounded. The cars jerked. We were off, screaming!

1. Which story made you feel as if you were there? Why? _____
_____

2. Which person do you feel you know better? Why? _____
_____

3. Which person showed more feelings? How? _____
_____
_____

Week 5 • Day 2

 **Voice** — Write honestly. Use your unique writing voice to let your reader get to know the real you.

A. Read Lizzie's story. Write the missing commas.

Puzzling Pizza

Grandma asked me to stay for lunch the other day. "We're having homemade pizza" she said. "Call your mom and tell her."

Lunch was yummy. When I'd cleaned my plate, I asked for another slice. "This pizza is the best!" I exclaimed.

Grandma grinned. "I'm glad you like it" she said. "I didn't have enough tomato sauce, so I blended carrots and sweet potatoes with some tomatoes."

My eyes opened wide. I couldn't believe that I had eaten carrots and sweet potatoes! I hate those foods. But you know what, that pizza was really good! "You're a great cook, Grandma" I admitted.

B. What would you think and say if you were served carrot and sweet potato pizza? Write two sentences in each bubble. Use your own voice.

Week 5 • Day 3

 **Voice** — Keep your reader interested by showing who you really are.

Read each situation. What would you say if it happened to you? Be sure to use your own unique voice.

1. If I saw a dinosaur peeking around the corner, I'd say…

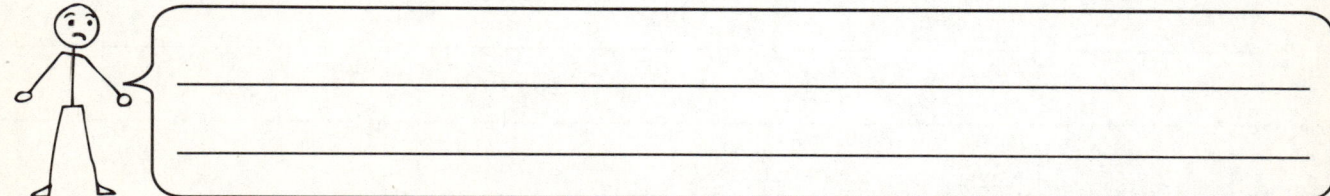

2. If my friend fell down and got hurt, I'd say…

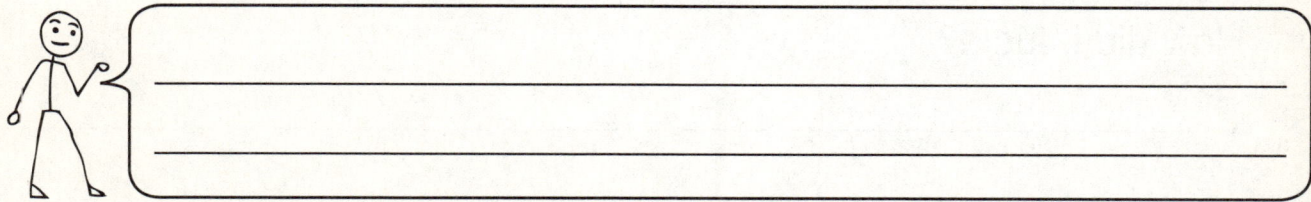

3. If I found out I had to go to a different school, I'd say…

4. If I met a talking cat, I'd say…

Week 5 • Day 4

 **Voice** — Use your unique writing voice to tell about a personal experience.

Think about the first time you tried an interesting or unusual food. What did you say? What did you do? Write your ideas.

Type of food: _____

What did it look like?
_____
_____

How did you feel about it before you tasted it?
_____
_____

Why did you taste it?
_____

How did it taste?
_____

How did you feel about the food after you tasted it?
_____
_____

What did you say?
_____
_____

Week 5 • Day 5

 Write about a time you tried a food for the first time. Let your own voice come out in your writing.

Be sure to place commas before quotation marks in dialogue.

Proofreading Marks

Mark	Meaning	Example
Ꝺ	Take this out (delete).	I love ~~to~~ to read.
⊙	Add a period.	It was late⊙
≡	Make this a capital letter.	First prize went to m̲≡aria.
/	Make this a lowercase letter.	We saw a B/lack C/at.
——	Fix the spelling.	This is our ~~hause~~ house.
∧ (comma)	Add a comma.	Goodnight∧ Mom.
⋎	Add an apostrophe.	That⋎s Lil⋎s bike.
!∧ ?∧	Add an exclamation point or a question mark.	Help!∧ Can you help me?∧
∧	Add a word or a letter.	The ∧red pen is mine.
#∧	Add a space between words.	I like#∧pizza.
——	Underline the words.	We read <u>Old Yeller</u>.
⋎ " ⋎ "	Add quotation marks.	⋎"Come in,⋎" he said.